THE CONSCIOUS INVESTOR® METHOD

3 steps to identify great share market investments

KEITH FOREMAN

The Conscious Investor® Method
3 steps to identify great share market investments

ISBN: 978-1-922644-44-2 (Hardcover)
978-1-922644-32-9 (Paperback)
978-1-922644-33-6 (eBook)

NATIONAL LIBRARY OF AUSTRALIA

A catalogue record for this book is available from the National Library of Australia

Editors: Kristy Martin and Jason Martin
Cover Design: Keith Foreman and Ocean Reeve Publishing
Design and Typeset: Ocean Reeve Publishing
Printed in Australia by Ocean Reeve Publishing

Published by Keith Foreman and Ocean Reeve Publishing
www.oceanreevepublishing.com

Ocean REEVE PUBLISHING

Foreword

Keith Foreman joined Teaminvest® in 2011 and has since become a valued master coach helping hundreds of Teaminvest members get the most from their membership by identifying Wealth Winners®. Finding similarities between investing and his experience as a fixed-wing and helicopter pilot, Keith eloquently describes how he manages his own portfolio using the Conscious Investor® application and the Teaminvest approach.

While Keith has benefitted by applying the tips and methods that are described throughout the book, he does encourage readers to draw on their own experiences and business acumen when investing.

Some background information on the origins of Conscious Investor® has been appended at the end of the book.

Dr John Price
Developer of Conscious Investor®
and a founder of Teaminvest

Disclaimer

My motivation to write this book is to assist fellow investors to improve their investments by using the methodology described. As an investor, I am sure you will understand that neither I, nor anyone else, can predict what the future holds.

The methodology relies a great deal on past performance to provide a guide for the future without defining a level of success. If a business has been successful in the past, the chances are it will continue to be successful, especially if the same management remains in place.

This book does not provide any financial advice or stock tips and should only be considered an educational and information resource.

My intention is to help you identify future Wealth Winners® and avoid Capital Killers™.

Your own results will depend on how your emotions are managed and how diligently you follow the methodology as outlined. Outcomes will also vary depending on personal experience, background, and, of course, market sentiment.

Please bear in mind the methodology applies only to long-term investing (at least five years) which, therefore, excludes short-term trading.

Readers should undertake their own due diligence and satisfy themselves in relation to the material presented and any companies discussed.

Readers should also be aware that I may own shares in one or more of the businesses mentioned.

Trademarks

The following terms are registered trademarks and are used with permission: Conscious Investor®, Wealth Winner®, STRETD®, TARGD®, Staegr®.

Table of Contents

Table of Figures

Acknowledgements

As with most endeavours, it is difficult for a person to succeed on their own. There are a number of people I am most grateful to for their kind assistance and support, and I wish to publicly thank them for all their contributions. Sheri Foreman, my wonderful wife, who supported my quest and devoted herself to helping me review my book; Kelly Law for providing invaluable insights and considerable time; Cadeyrn Gaskin for deeper perceptions; George Stoopin and Peter Richardson for checking the numbers; Sue and Mark Rallings; Julie Pereira and Michelle Chipreo; and Kristy Martin, Jason Smith, Jason Martin, and Marisa Parker from Ocean Reeve Publishing.

A mention must be made of Warren Buffett who has greatly inspired me from an early age. He is recognised as not only one of the greatest investors of our time but also as an exceptional human being.

I am deeply indebted to Dr John Price for his mentorship and to the founders of Teaminvest, Howard Coleman and Mark Moreland, for their guidance and insights and for allowing me to share their CI methodology with you. I encourage you to read John and Howard's excellent book *Finding Wealth Winners® the Teaminvest Way*.

Dedication

Since my early teens, I have had an enduring interest in property investing, business, and the share market. Fortunately, as a consistently good saver, it afforded me the means to actively participate in these interests.

Out of the three investment classes, I found success in the share market the most elusive, and my returns erratic, until in 2011 when I joined Teaminvest, 'a private membership organisation for those who wish to educate themselves to manage their wealth wisely, rather than paying others to do it badly for them'.

The Conscious Investor® ('CI') methodology was adopted by Teaminvest, and this, along with their clearly articulated processes, helped me to significantly improve my returns, which in turn has given me greater confidence and comfort along my investing journey.

In my ongoing quest to help other share investors who are treading the same path, I dedicate this book to you and trust it will give you the best possibility of success in your future investments.

About the Author

Keith spent his formative years on a large game ranch in Zimbabwe, where he gained a lifelong passion for flying from his father, who had painstakingly rebuilt his own WWII biplane trainer, a Tiger Moth. Not surprisingly, as soon as Keith turned eighteen, he obtained his pilot's license, progressing to become an instructor, then a commercial helicopter pilot. He combined his passion for aviation and business by flying international clients to the 20,000-acre game ranch, teeming with wildlife. With the increasing interest in observing animals in their natural environment, Keith became instrumental in helping his father build up the safari side of their family business.

While studying computer science at university in the 1980s, Keith's elective subjects of economics and psychology sparked an interest in both property and share-market investing.

Under the guidance of a learned uncle, Keith made his first share investments. As he progressively gained a deeper insight into investing and behavioural finance, he began to see similarities between flying and investing, in both mind-set and the management of risk. Keith has distinguished himself in these endeavours.

Keith coaches Teaminvest* members on how to benefit most from CI. He also enjoys interactions with fellow investors and relishes the inherent culture of knowledge sharing. Keith also spends many weekends in the cockpit, flying clients into wineries for lunch or along the beautiful Gold Coast.

His insatiable drive to assist others in achieving their investment goals inspired him to write this book, which explains the CI methodology and processes adopted by Teaminvest as they seek to find great investment opportunities at a reasonable price.

**A private investment organisation.*

Preface

There seems to be some perverse human characteristic that likes to make easy things difficult.[1]

—Warren Buffett

This quote from Warren Buffett was my prime motivator in writing this book—to make it simpler and easier for any person to invest in the share market. By following a clear step-by-step methodology, and by avoiding the hype around share investing, we are better placed to reap the rewards. During my coaching sessions with hundreds of Teaminvest members, I have come to realise that I'm in a unique position to share the knowledge and personal experience I have gained over time. In this way, I feel able to help my fellow investors reach for their own financial goals.

I have personally spent over forty years searching for a straightforward investing method. It began as a teenager when I became fascinated with the alluring stories about Wall Street. By good fortune, I turned to my uncle—a successful investor himself—who nurtured my growing interest. We discussed at length the internal workings of businesses and how to select those that would prevail, even in market downturns. As this was before the days of Google and online investing, I became proficient at reading the daily financial papers and understanding the value of the information they provided.

I was raring to go, and when I had accumulated some savings, I invested in a gold business listed on the South African stock exchange. For two years, I applied myself to my studies at university and, after graduating, I married my fiancée and needed some money for our honeymoon. Remembering my gold shares, I decided to cash them in and was amazed that they had nearly doubled in price. Wow! How easy was that?

Buoyed by my success, I then entered a share trading competition and was the very delighted winner. The Johannesburg stock exchange in South Africa was an economic powerhouse at the time, so I felt considerable pride in being flown down there and fêted for the day. My confidence soared and I dived headlong into the share market. Pride does indeed come before a fall, and only *then* did I realise I still had so much to learn.

With my dual passions of helicopter flying and share investing, I began to realise how easy, yet dangerous, overconfidence could be. A popular warning to pilots is:

> *When you've flown 100 hours you think you know everything.*
> *When you reach 1,000 hours you know you know everything.*
> *When you've attained 10,000 hours, you realise you'll never know everything.*

During my early years in share investing, I tried my hand at many strategies, including day trading, options, contracts for difference, and technical analysis—with mixed results. I slowly but surely learned that long-term investing is, for me, the safest, steadiest method to achieve consistently good returns.

When the first major drop of the global financial crisis (GFC) occurred, I panicked and sold my entire portfolio in a day. The shock of the GFC fallout motivated me to become a safer investor and my research led me to joining Teaminvest. The philosophy of the company and regular interactions with a learned and experienced group of members came as a revelation. I completely immersed myself in the process and progressively became a more confident and knowledgeable investor. Once I began coaching members on the CI application and methodology, I realised that business acumen did not automatically translate to share investing prowess. This motivated me to put pen to paper in order to share my own investing journey and provide encouragement to my readers.

As you continue reading, you might notice I often quote Warren Buffett—the world's best-known and most successful long-term investor. I make no apology for this, as his common sense and practical methods have influenced my long-term investing journey.

Introduction

Wouldn't it be an ideal scenario to follow a simple set of guidelines to find great businesses to invest in and to know the most sensible price to pay when purchasing?

Throughout this book, I aim to achieve just this by demonstrating the Teaminvest Way and CI methodology as created by John Price.

The Teaminvest Way reflects the overarching principles of fundamental analysis combined with the collaboration of like-minded investors.

The CI methodology features three distinct steps:

- Filter
- Research
- Buy with a margin of safety (MOS).

It has taken me a while—forty years in fact—to feel absolutely confident in my investing strategy. I am highly motivated to save time for you, my fellow investors, by introducing a methodology that is simple, common sense and, if followed with diligence, should certainly improve your investment results.

A manageable portfolio could consist of fifteen to twenty great businesses which have been identified and then purchased at a sensible price. It would be reasonable to set a goal of achieving a return of at least 15% per annum over the long term. As a point of reference, the 30-year average return per annum of the ASX® Accumulation Index is 10.1%.

In the pages to follow, I have detailed the process we adopt at Teaminvest, along with many of my own individual experiences, some of which were challenging and, at times, painful. I have also shared insights from a decade of interactions with Teaminvest members.

Below is a brief summary of the chapters:

- **PART 1: Chapter 1** focuses on the required mindset, exploring human biases and how events can influence us to react impulsively and, often, emotionally.
- **PART 2: Chapter 2** introduces the key financial statements and the relevant ratios. I use a case study of Australian vehicle accessory manufacturer ARB Corporation Ltd to illustrate these in practice, particularly as their financials are straightforward and therefore easier to understand.
- **PART 3: Chapters 3–10** the methodology:
- **Chapter 3** describes the CI methodology to find great businesses, with good prospects, and how to purchase them at a sensible price. This is achieved by following the three distinct steps.
- **Chapter 4**
  Step 1: identify businesses with strong financials with the help of the CI filter. This results in approximately sixty businesses out of the 2,288 currently listed on the ASX.
- **Chapters 5–9**
  Step 2: assess the businesses with good management and evaluate the business risks and economic moats (unique product or service). This further refines the sixty businesses down to thirty that are worthy of consideration in Step 3.

- **Chapter 10**
  Step 3: how to establish a sensible price to pay for any of the remaining thirty businesses and place orders accordingly.
  Think of these steps as a stool with three legs—if one is missing, the stool topples.
- **PART 4: Chapter 11:** Buying is easy, and selling is hard, so I devote an entire chapter to letting go.
- **PART 5: Chapter 12** summarises the methodology and the steps involved.

I wrote this book so that each chapter is a building block for the next one; refer to Figure 1 on the next page.

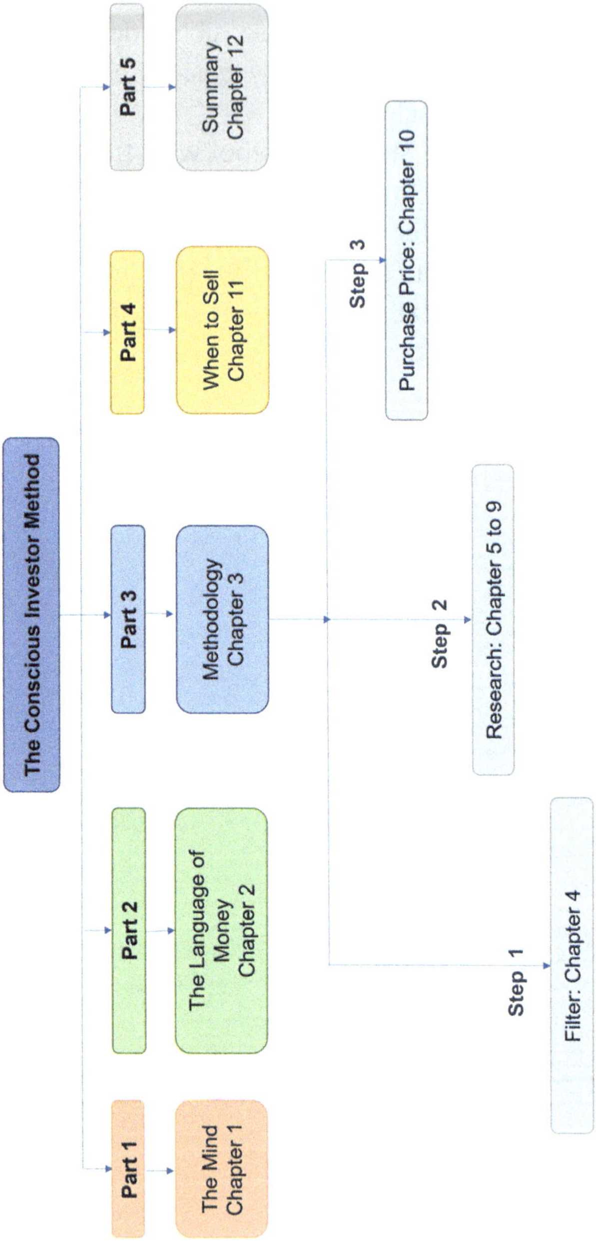

Figure 1—Breakdown of chapters

I enjoy reading a wide variety of business and investing books and articles and will never stop learning.

'Without Warren Buffett being a learning machine—a continuous learning machine—the [outstanding long-term] record would have been absolutely impossible.'[2]

In Appendix 5, I share a list of my own recommended reading.

Some documents and linked references reside in a password-protected website. These may only be accessible to Teaminvest members. If you are interested in finding out more, please visit: www.teaminvest.com.au.

For further reading on these principles, *Finding Wealth Winners® the Teaminvest Way* is a series of letters and articles by Howard Coleman and John Price.

I hope you will find my book helpful, as well as interesting, and trust it will provide you with the confidence to invest in the share market for your future financial security.

It's important to highlight that I describe my personal experiences and express my own opinions. As such, the content is intended solely for information and educational purposes. Please undertake your own due diligence.

> *Please note that all Teaminvest material (logo, quotes, images, statistics, and so on) is reproduced with the permission of Teaminvest.*

Part 1

MINDSET

Chapter 1
The Mind

I start with the mind in mind. Why? Well, if we are going to be successful in our own investing, it helps to understand right up front that, as with most worthwhile endeavours, share investing will test our resolve and trigger many human biases, our understanding of our emotions, and how we react to greed and fear.

It's all well and good to follow the methodology with the idea that we are always rational and can feasibly make profitable investment decisions. However, studies of behavioural finance highlight some human characteristics that challenge this premise. It is difficult to control our feelings when investing, as humans are susceptible to certain trends and subconsciously influenced by the stories and thoughts of others. We are all hardwired to take shortcuts and are often over-confident with our decisions.

The CI methodology provides a clear and logical framework that assists in minimising rash decisions influenced by emotions. Following this approach will give you the confidence to stay true to the process. A level of commitment is required as those who 'have a go' or 'dabble' in the share market are unlikely to succeed.

Because good businesses take time to grow, it is wise to commit any capital outlay for at least 5–10 years. Only consider selling when the business no longer meets your original criteria for buying.

Teaminvest members take a long-term view on investing and, as the share market is volatile, there is always an associated element of risk. When committing our capital to the share market, we cannot avoid risk, so we need to manage it. Everyone reacts to risk differently, so it is important to understand our own susceptibility to it.

Too often, the mind primarily influences investors' actions. For a more in-depth understanding of how money and emotions are inextricably linked, you may enjoy reading *Your Money and Your Brain* by Jason Zweig (2007).

Charlie Munger has produced a list of twenty-five human tendencies that are truly relevant to investing in the share market. I keep a copy of *Poor Charlie's Almanack* nearby because, aside from addressing our tendencies and biases, it is also full of useful, informative, and witty comments.[3]

An observation about mindset comes from the legendary former manager of the Magellan Fund, Peter Lynch: 'Everyone has the brainpower to make money in stocks. Not everyone has the stomach.'[4]

No-one likes to admit to making a bad investment decision, and we may even protect our own egos by not selling out of a failing business promptly. Success in investing is not only about buying into good businesses, but also about purchasing shares at a sensible price and selling them when they no longer fit our original buying criteria.

Our human emotions and biases can undermine a logical assessment of a business. Be wary of falling in love with any investment and becoming distracted by daily price movements. Rather, focus on how well earnings are growing as, in time, the share price is sure to follow.

An investor will succeed by coupling good business judgement with an ability to insulate his thoughts and behaviour from the super-contagious emotions that swirl about the marketplace.[5]

—Buffett (Shareholder Letters 1987)

Mindset Required

Mindset is a vast subject, and I have focused on just four areas of awareness:

- Reactions to risk
- Ability to remain patient
- Commitment to learning
- Emotions.

Reactions to risk

Benjamin Graham said, 'The investor's chief problem, and even his worst enemy, is likely to be himself.'[6]

We need to understand ourselves, acknowledge our limitations, and decide how best to deal with them. We are hardwired from birth and are here because our ancestors were incredibly good at identifying potential danger and avoiding it. While risk avoidance was instrumental to their survival, the same aversion to risk may not be helpful in the world of investing.

We should recognise this deeply human trait of avoiding risk and become aware of our emotions and inherent biases when managing our share portfolios. They can dramatically affect our decision-making. Most investors perceive volatility (large daily movements of the share price) as a risk but, with a better understanding, we could consider it an opportunity.

Perhaps ask yourself how you react to feelings of anger and frustration as well as to excitement and elation. Then transpose these feelings to the realm of investing with its inevitable financial losses and gains. Might you jump to conclusions and overreact or bury your head in the sand and take no action at all?

One useful technique to assess how you might react is to simulate a situation, both desirable and undesirable, before it may occur.

It's a good idea to assess how you might feel and react if a particular *event* were to occur. Visualise, for instance, having a significant amount of capital invested in the share market and your reaction if the market dropped by 50%, as occurred in the GFC, or even 37%, as it has due to the COVID-19 pandemic. The more mentally prepared you are, the better your decision-making will be.

Every time I go flying, I take a few minutes to prepare myself physically and emotionally should I experience an engine failure. This is to ensure I would act instinctively as my muscle memory is more likely to manage my actions for a successful outcome. So far, I have survived four engine failures in my flying career!

The media hype around investments such as bitcoin and other speculative businesses can be an unhelpful distraction. Media noise is almost impossible to avoid and certainly affects our mindset. My advice here is to follow your very specific investment strategy to improve your chances of maintaining focus and avoiding distraction.

When considering what separates the best sportspeople from the rest of the pack, most often the individual's success is due to mindset, their focus, and determination, just as much as superior skills.

I recognise upfront that I am no different from anyone else and am acutely aware of the human biases affecting my own decisions. I try to mitigate them by:

- Developing the right mindset for investing.
- Sticking closely to the CI methodology.
- Not being distracted or influenced by external factors or opinions.

Ability to remain patient

The key feature from the mindset perspective is *patience:* try not to rush into buying into a business at too high a price and, once purchased, allow time for the power of compounding to work.

You may have heard the term 'the magic of compounding'. It's easier to explain with an example, so let's take a hypothetical round of golf (eighteen holes). I go to the course with a mate and suggest playing for just ten cents per hole—my fellow golfer scoffs at this small wager. I then suggest we double up after each hole, and my mate agrees, not realising the compounding ramifications. Take a guess at how much we will be playing for on the last hole. Do you expect it to be $5 or $60, or even $1,000? Wait for it—it is actually $13,107.20.

Hole 1	0.10
Hole 2	0.20
Hole 3	0.40
Hole 4	0.80
Hole 5	1.60
Hole 6	3.20
Hole 7	6.40
Hole 8	12.80
Hole 9	25.60
Hole 10	51.20
Hole 11	102.40
Hole 12	204.80
Hole 13	409.60
Hole 14	819.20
Hole 15	1,638.40
Hole 16	3,276.80
Hole 17	6,553.60
Hole 18	13,107.20

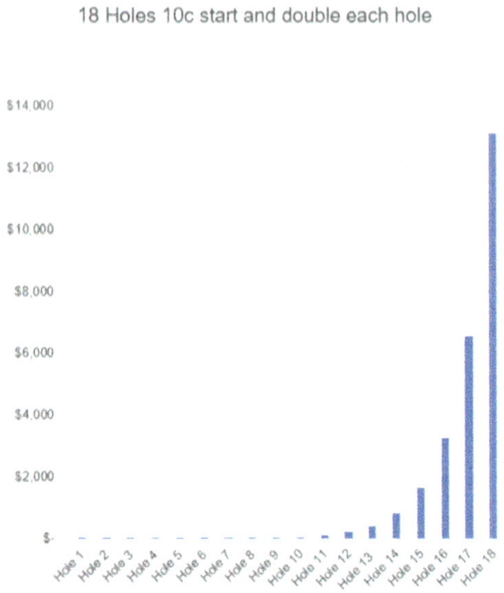

Table 1—The result of compounding

And remember, we started off with just ten cents.

Compound interest is the greatest mathematical discovery of all time.[7]

Let the above example reinforce how compounding gains in momentum the more the principal is left untouched. In the same way, patience with our investments will more likely deliver the returns we seek with minimum input from ourselves. Wealth in the share market comes from capital growth plus dividends, and we must allow both to work in our favour.

Commitment to learning

Many people don't want to be beholden to others when it comes to managing our personal investments.

Self-education is key to our confidence and level of knowledge, and we can benefit by committing to reading the annual reports of companies in our portfolio, as well as any books in the 'Recommended Reading' section in Appendix 5.

As you're probably aware, the Royal Commission into Misconduct in the Banking, Superannuation and Financial Services Industry (December 2017 to February 2019) laid bare how unethical some financial planners and advisors had been in the past. This reinforced my own commitment to continual learning and accountability for my personal investing outcomes. My wife and investing partner, Sheri, and I stay abreast of our investment activities and keep detailed records, just as we would expect a professional financial advisor to do. We attend the annual general meetings (AGMs) for the businesses we are interested or invested in, and dedicate time and effort in reading company reports and conducting thorough research.

For my own portfolio transactions, I utilise an online broker and an online portfolio tracking application. As a member of Teaminvest, I also access the CI software application which scans the ASX and many other global markets, helping me identify the businesses that pass a range of filters (for example: consistent earnings and sales over a five-year period, low debt, and consistent returns on equity), thus narrowing down my search to a manageable number of potential investments.

Aware of emotions

Some strong emotions may override our logic. These emotions will impact our investing decisions, yet we often don't even consider them. Let's look at the fear of missing out (FOMO).

FOMO might come into play when a business passes the first two steps of assessment in the CI methodology, namely where members ask:

1. Does the business have strong financials?
2. Is there good management and deep moats, and have we assessed the risks?

Once the assessment is complete, there is usually a strong urge to skip the important third step of buying at a sensible price. Even once a business has passed the hurdles and criteria, it's important to employ restraint if the share price is too expensive at the time. To avoid FOMO, patience and discipline are required in waiting for a sensible price to be reached, or rather a fair price to earnings ratio ('PE'), and only then buy shares in the business.

Although the PE is expanded on later, it is important to introduce the concept now. As a general rule, when purchasing shares, the lower the PE, the better. This confirms that a purchase is being made at a fair price. The PE is a stock's price divided by its earnings.

The PE ratio effectively reveals how many years' worth of earnings per share will match the current share price, assuming the earnings remain flat.

Other strong emotions which, incidentally, affect our daily lives are:

- Comparing ourselves to others
- Being influenced by our peers.

Human Biases

Biases also have the potential to impact our investing.

- Loss aversion
- Confirmation
- Recency
- Groupthink
- Information
- Oversimplification tendency
- Anchoring
- Restraint.

Loss aversion

Humans feel the effects of pain far more than they do pleasure, which served our ancestors well and contributed to why you and I are here today. However, in share investing, we may find ourselves unable to accept a loss when share prices fall considerably. We are reluctant to sell until the price climbs back to its original level. Dr John Price refers to this as 'get-even-itis'. There are two potential scenarios at play:

1. Investors may be reluctant to sell and crystallise their losses and, to avoid the pain, they hold on.
2. Investors panic at witnessing the losses mounting and sell impulsively to avoid further pain.

In both cases, it is preferable to take into consideration the strength of the business and its fundamentals. If the business is sound, an investor could instead take advantage of the opportunity to add to their holdings. Conversely, if the fundamentals are in question, then the investor can justify selling immediately.

The challenge is to discern if specific events constitute a threat or opportunity to the business and to then react in a timely manner.

Loss aversion is an extraordinarily strong human emotion, and a mounting loss can cause considerable distress. Daniel Kahneman, the Nobel prize winner, has revealed humans feel twice as much emotion over a financial loss than a financial win.

To understand this 2:1 emotion ratio further, let's say we had five businesses in our portfolio, and two are in a loss situation.

Our overall *negative* feeling is 4, being 2 shares x pain weighting of 2.

The remaining three businesses in our portfolio are in a positive situation, so our overall *positive* feeling is 3, being 3 shares x pleasure weighting of 1.

The intensified feeling of a loss affects us more than the euphoria of a gain. Market fluctuations will inevitably invoke emotions, so keep a firm focus on the long term.

Confirmation bias

We tend to take more notice of information conforming to our thinking, ignoring contradictory information. This results in confirmation bias. As an example, if we invested in a health business, we could lean towards reading information actively supporting the industry, and hence believe both the business and the industry will perform better than they actually may.

When thinking of buying a particular car, suddenly we notice them everywhere when out driving.

Confirmation bias can easily lead to becoming overconfident with the businesses we have invested in, especially if we only absorb a positive view of them. A helpful way to manage this bias is to adopt a more contrarian outlook and consider a less favourable scenario.

As Charlie Munger has said, 'We all are learning, modifying, or destroying ideas all the time. Rapid destruction of your ideas when the time is right is one of the most valuable qualities you can acquire. You must force yourself to consider arguments on the other side'.[8]

Recency bias

We all tend to focus on the most recent events. As hunter-gatherers roaming the plains, the leopard looking at us right now poses a far greater threat than the one we saw last week. Placing more relevance on the most recent information at the expense of earlier information, regardless of importance, is called recency bias.

For example, a business's latest interim report could show an excellent performance, despite the mediocre results of the previous four years. Do we automatically assume it will continue?

As I write, we are in the midst of the COVID-19 pandemic and it is dominating the news, as is the reportedly *unprecedented* volatility in the share market.

To put it into perspective, look at the next chart depicting the CBOE® Volatility Index (VIX) from the last twenty years. As you can see, the volatility as of May 2020 is actually 10.6% less than at the peak of the GFC. We forget quite easily the feeling of uncertainty, and resulting market volatility, the world experienced during major events such as the outbreak of the Iraq war (2003).

Figure 2—CBOE Volatility Index (VIX) [9]

Groupthink bias

Have you heard the phrase 'jump on the bandwagon'? It's used to describe the support of a cause that's fashionable or considered to be successful. When it comes to survival in the wild, there is often safety in numbers so there is merit in moving together in a herd.

However, in the realm of investing, this herd mentality is called groupthink. It implies to us that the individuals aren't thinking.

It is a fundamental human trait to be agreeable to bond with each other and avoid conflict. We feel much more comfortable when others share the same viewpoint as ourselves. However, to avoid groupthink, acknowledge and debate other views at the same time as doing independent research so ultimately, you can make your own informed decisions.

The benefit of Teaminvest is that purchase or sale of a business is left entirely to the individual member.

Information bias

The best example of information bias I can give is how the media influences us. These days, we are so often overwhelmed with information it's difficult to determine what is best to read or listen to. It is equally hard to distil what information is simply untrue or irrelevant. We should constantly remind ourselves that 'bad news sells'.

Some investment articles may focus on changes to a business's share price, which is driven by market sentiment, as opposed to any factual changes in the status of the business. When there is a sharp drop in a share price, there is a strong tendency to think *they* know something you do not, and you may give the information undue credence. Be wary of tag lines like 'it's different this time' or labels such as the 'Resources Super Cycle' or 'Peak Oil'. Focus on the business fundamentals and prospects instead.

Our tendency to crave certainty is why we are so naturally drawn to *expert* predictions. However, at the end of the day, no-one has more proof of future trends or outcomes than anyone else.

Researchers David Bailey and collaborators analysed a dataset of 6,627 forecasts made by sixty-eight forecasters from 1998 to 2005. The outcome was only a 48% accuracy in their forecasting, a result not significantly different to chance. Further explanations can be found in the chapter 'Forecasting and the Three Most Important Words in Investing' from John Price's book *The Conscious Investor*®.[10]

Paul Slovic, a Professor of Psychology at the University of Oregon, ran an interesting experiment on information bias. He sought out the best eight-horse handicappers in America who derive their living from horse racing. He then provided each handicapper with seventy-five pieces of information spread over four races.

In the first race, they could choose any *five* pieces of information, for example, a horse's name, weight, and previous wins. In the second race, they could choose *ten* more pieces of information. In the third race, they received *twenty* further pieces of information and in the final race, handicappers were provided with all the remaining information.

With ten horses competing at a time, the handicappers had a minimum 10% chance of picking the winner in each race. Paul measured their expected results against their confidence levels during each race.

After the first race, he noted a 17% success rate and a 19% confidence level. In other words, the handicappers' ability to choose a winner more or less matched their confidence. With every subsequent race, their confidence grew with the increase in the information they received.

Interestingly, however, the handicappers' results did not improve. This little story illustrates that more information does not necessarily return better results.[11]

Oversimplification tendency

In satisfying our craving for certainty, we prefer things to be simple and clear. Modern technology has made our lives much easier as we can now swiftly access a shortlist of quality businesses via a scanning application such as CI. If we were to rely entirely on this list, we might fall prey to oversimplification tendency. We should, therefore, commit to taking the time and effort to also undertake a qualitative analysis of the businesses (Step 2).

As Einstein supposedly said: 'Make everything as simple as possible, but not simpler.'[12]

Anchoring bias

In investing, we can anchor by being unwilling to cut our losses when one of our businesses is not performing to expectation. For example, we could purchase shares in a business for $30 which then falls by 33% to $20. Even if the fundamentals deteriorate, which should trigger the action to sell, we are still reluctant to do so until the price reverts to the $30 we initially paid. This attachment to our investments could become our folly and serve to hinder long-term investing success.

Focus instead on the fundamentals and future prospects of the business and whether there is any realistic hope of recovery, or if we are likely to erode more of our capital by holding on.

Restraint bias

Restraint bias could be experienced by an investor who has a solid investing plan allowing for equal monetary commitments to each new share purchase. This could be a useful strategy for new investors to manage their investable capital.

A perceived bargain then presents itself, and the investor impulsively breaks his rules and buys well above his predefined allocation on the single purchase.

The lack of self-control has led to a greater exposure to temptation which this investor was unable to resist.

Restraint bias is the confidence that resistance is possible.

Chapter Summary

I trust these insights have given you an appreciation of why I started this book with the mind. If we do not have the right mindset and recognise our human biases, we will find the whole investing process frustrating and stressful.

Activity: Take a moment now to identify how you react to risk, how patient you are and how aware of your emotions when investing. Look at one personal example of how prone you have been in the past to each of the biases discussed (loss aversion, confirmation, recency, groupthink, information, oversimplification tendency, anchoring, restraint). Analyse some poor investing decisions you have made in the past and make a note in your investing diary if any of them were caused by one of these biases.

Notes

....

....

....

....

....

....

....

....

....

....

....

....

....

....

Part 2

UNDERSTANDING THE FINANCIALS

Chapter 2
Accounting—The Language of Business and Finance

According to Warren Buffett, 'Accounting is the language of business.'[13]

The more you understand the financials, the better you will understand the business. To this end, we can thank the wonderful world of technology and financial ratios for the assistance they provide.

Accounting is not the be-all and end-all of investing, but it provides a scorecard to judge how well a business is doing. Dean Robinson, CFO of Teaminvest Private Group Limited, relates accounting to a cricket game where the scoreboard provides the figures, and the captain (CEO) manages the strategy, fielders, and bowlers. The energy and dedication of the players, under direction from their captain, can have a greater impact on the result of the game than the scoreboard may indicate.

The three main financial statements—balance sheet, profit and loss statement, and cash flow statement—will now be explored to provide you with a guide to analysing the key financial ratios in step 1 of the CI methodology.

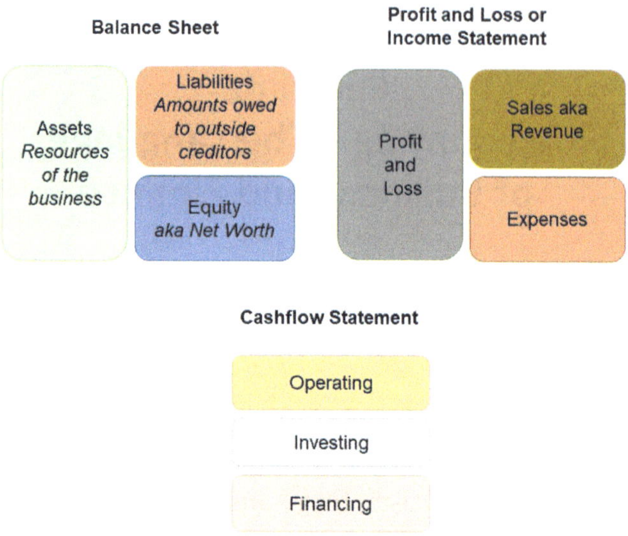

Figure 3—The key components of the financial statements

The Balance Sheet

The balance sheet reflects a business's financial position (assets, liabilities, and equity). It is a snapshot of figures as at the end of the reporting period, or at a specified point in time.

The Profit and Loss Statement

The profit and loss (or income) statement details how much money has been made or lost during the reporting period. This is all the income earned by the business, less the expenses incurred in achieving those earnings.

The Cash Flow Statement

The cash flow statement reflects what cash has come into and out of the business during the reporting period.

As a reminder, ARB has been selected as my sample business due to its simple and clearly articulated financial reports. This should assist you in understanding the reports, the language of finance and associated financial ratios preferred by Teaminvest. It is helpful to download a full copy of the latest annual report from their website: <www.arb.com.au>. Detailed breakdowns of the three financial statements can be found in Appendix 1 and they can be downloaded for free from the Teaminvest website via this link: **<www.teaminvest.com.au/how-to-use-conscious-investor>**.

I suggest printing them out to refer to when reading this book and I will endeavour to keep them updated on this link, following each reporting period.

My own returns undoubtedly improved by studying trends within the financial statements and following up with immediate research on any anomalies found. For example, if a business should change its method of reporting from one annual report to the next, I would wonder what it might be trying to hide or portray.

It is important to know that the annual report can, quite legally, be presented in a way that:

- Makes the management and board look good.
- Appeases its lenders (probably a bank).
- Pleases its shareholders.

Remain alert to any noticeable changes in the most recent financial statements. Often, government regulatory requirements can cause significant changes in accounting procedures. There are two recent examples. Firstly, the cost impact of the Minerals Resource Rent Tax on mining service businesses (keenly felt by the company Mineral Resources) and secondly, the disclosure impact of the new AASB 16 ruling, where long-term property leases are required to be included in the balance sheet. This has particularly impacted retailers with a large number of outlets, such as Super Retail Group.

By reading a good number of business annual reports, your familiarity and understanding of their construction will certainly improve. Start with the ARB report, being one of the simplest, and then progress to other businesses you hold shares in.

With each report read, you will gain more insight into how the business makes its money, how its executives are rewarded (detailed in the remuneration report), and how its finances are reported. My personal preference is to obtain a hard copy of the annual reports so I can highlight anomalies and add my own notes.

Introductions have been made, and we will be delving further into the CI methodology which encompasses management, earnings outlook, moats, and risks.

Chapter Summary

I have provided an overview of the key financial statements that an Australian business produces every six months. More detailed analysis is provided in Appendix 1, along with the key ratios and the suggested benchmarks.

Activity: Study the financial statements of a business in which you own shares and write down any questions that come up as a result. As a shareholder, you may call the investor relations personnel of any business to raise any concerns you may have.

As a reminder, the ARB financials are available on the website: **<www.teaminvest.com.au/how-to-use-conscious-investor>**. In Appendix 1, I have shown each financial ratio we use and how they are derived and referenced them to ARB's financials. Take time to review this as a case study and then apply to your own investments.

Notes

....

....

....

....

....

....

....

....

....

....

....

....

....

....

Part 3

THE METHODOLOGY

Chapter 3
Three Distinct Steps

The CI methodology comprises of three distinct steps:

1. Filter on financials
2. Research
3. Purchase price.

Filter on Financials

By applying the filter in the CI application, with the criteria detailed in Chapter 4, we can obtain a list of businesses with sound financials.

The criteria are:

- Strong and stable growth in earnings and sales.
- High and consistent return on equity, above 10%.
- Minimal debt (debt to equity less than 50%).

A further refinement of this list of businesses is made at a triage meeting which follows the six-monthly release of financial results. The knowledge and expertise of the members is then shared to weed out any businesses not worth spending time and effort on. On average, the resultant list contains about thirty-five businesses from which investors might select about fifteen to twenty for their own portfolios.

Note: Share price is not considered at any time during Step 1.

Research

With the short list from Step 1, we will now look in more detail at management and whether their remuneration incentives align with the growth of the business, which is of particular interest to shareholders. We also assess the individual moats and risks for a deeper understanding of each business and to assist in predicting its future earnings.

Qualitative measures to be considered for each business: how does the business actually make money? What is its business model and the drivers for their products or services? What is the outlook for the business, and are there any tailwinds that could help performance? Look in more detail at management and whether their remuneration incentives align with the growth of the business and, in turn, the interests of shareholders. Assess the moats and risks that may pertain to each business.

Purchase Price

Should investors wish to purchase shares in any of these businesses, they can then consult the CI application. This assists in determining the maximum price to pay and enhances their confidence in achieving a required rate of return over the long term. There are inbuilt safety margins in the buy price calculations based on stress-testing key financial inputs.

As Warren Buffet says:

> *'Our method is very simple. We just try to buy businesses with good-to-superb underlying economics run by honest and able people and buy them at sensible prices. That's all I am trying to do.'*[14]

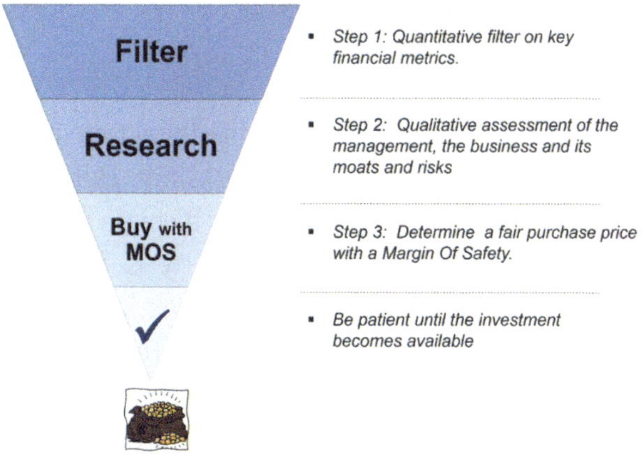

Figure 4—The three-step CI methodology

Let's explore the process further. The methodology may appear straightforward enough, so why do some investors fail to follow through? There could be three reasons:

Impatience

This is a result of being simply too eager to buy shares in the business, regardless of price, especially after doing all the hard work in Steps 1 and 2. We all experience a fear of missing out and become impatient as a result.

Taking shortcuts

This occurs when we are too easily influenced by other investors or rely on outcomes from an automated investment application without validating the information for ourselves.

Losing faith

This comes from abandoning the methodology when one or two investments do not perform as expected. We should remember that investing is not an exact science, and we can only depend on probabilities. A solid investing plan will be very valuable here.

Teaminvest aims to emulate the investing principles of Warren Buffett, chairman of Berkshire Hathaway. As of writing, the current share price for a single Class A (BRK.A) share is over $472,257. However, it is possible to buy Class B shares at a fraction of the cost, albeit with voting limitations. By purchasing BRK.B shares, we gain access to their annual and interim quarterly reports, including Warren Buffett's popular annual shareholder letter. His letters are sprinkled with his wonderful, folksy humour and they are both entertaining and hugely informative. I look forward to receiving them each year and read them multiple times. From Buffett's writings, we can glean valuable information about the man himself, his investing methods, and the investments he has made.

You may be wondering what kind of return you could reasonably expect from share market investing.

Dr John Price poses it as a question, 'What rate of return would you require to justify taking your capital out of the bank and investing it in the share market, with the associated risks?'

As a benchmark for any aspiring investor, I share the average returns of the All-Ordinaries Accumulation Index (the top 500 Australian Stock Exchange (ASX) businesses by market capitalisation, with dividends reinvested) below:

- 11.8% per annum over the last 120 years[15]
- 10.1% per annum for the last 30 years
- 7.9% per annum for the last 10 years.[16]

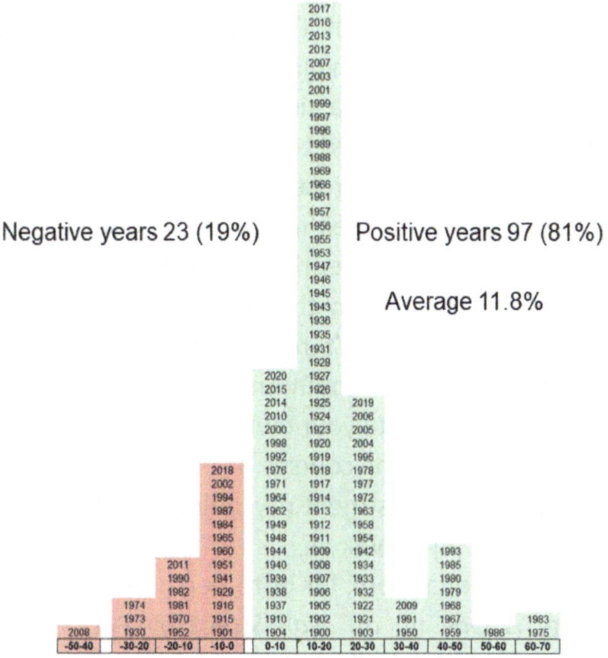

Figure 5—Returns of the Accumulation Index (XAOAI) over the last 120 years[16]

If we can achieve the 10-year average return of 7.9% per annum, and allow it to compound, our capital investment will double in 9.1 years. This would be a good starting point for most new investors, bearing in mind that past performance is not a reliable indicator of future performance.

Tip

A handy tool for estimating returns is the 'rule of 72': 72 (fixed figure) divided by 7.9 (% return) = 9.1 (years to double). In the same way, the 'rule of 115' applies to determine how many years it will take for our capital investment to triple, that is: 115 divided by 7.9 (% return) = 14.5 (years to triple).

To become familiar with the online broking process, I suggest committing the minimum amount (A$500) to make an initial purchase. It is a simple process and initial small purchases will help to build confidence for larger purchases. Some Australian online brokers allow us to purchase stocks on the US markets via their international trading platforms. The process is almost identical to purchasing on the ASX local market. Investing in the share market need not be intimidating as it doesn't require any formal education. However, patience and commitment are essential. Commit some time and effort to your own education. The ASX offers free introductory online courses. There are also many books on investing and investment psychology available—refer to my reading list (Appendix 5).

An inspirational book for both beginners and seasoned investors is *One up on Wall Street* by Peter Lynch. He retired in 1990, having grown the Fidelity Magellan Fund from $18 million in 1977 to $14 billion in 1990, a period of just thirteen years. Despite the fund falling by over 10% on numerous occasions during this time, he still managed an annual return of more than 29%. Encouragingly, Lynch asserts a private investor has just as much opportunity and access to information as a fund manager, with the benefit of less constraints on their trading activities.[17]

Peter Lynch taught me the importance of visiting business premises. At one stage, I owned shares in a popular pizza business and attended their AGM. The company's results were disappointing, as was the meeting overall. On the way home, I realised with some shame that I had no personal experience of their products. So, needing to eat, I downloaded their app and made an order! When I collected my pizza, I chatted to the owner, being surprised to learn they did not use one of the quality control cameras featured in their reports and media. When my pizza also disappointed, I decided to sell my shares. I have a personal need to be congruent with my investments and, unfortunately, the dots did not connect on this occasion.

Chapter Summary

Let's review the three-step CI methodology again:

Step 1: Filter

The criteria used in the filter will identify businesses that pass key financial ratios. The three main criteria are: stable and growing earnings and sales; return on equity; low levels of debt.

Share price is not considered at any time during Step 1.

Step 2: Research

There are several qualitative measures to be considered for each business. The quality of management, and their performance, is assessed as are the risks and moats of the business.

Step 3: Purchase price

If a business passes the scrutiny from the first two steps, then investors may choose to buy shares in any business that is within their circle of competence and is at a fair price or price earnings ratio (PE).

Activity: Start thinking about this methodology and how you can use it to purchase shares in a business in which you are interested.

Notes

Chapter 4
Step 1—The Filter

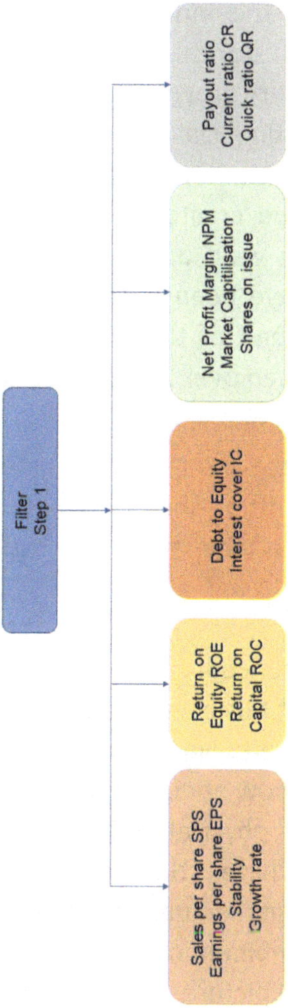

Figure 6—Key financial ratios

The use of an analytical application such as CI assists us by quickly and easily scanning and filtering the entire market of 2,288 currently listed businesses in Australia. The list that results from that scan should highlight businesses that pass the chosen criteria of key financial ratios. We seek businesses with a track record of over five years of audited results as this indicates robustness and validity. We also evaluate historical earnings and sales to assist in forecasting the future growth prospects of a business.

The validity of financial filters has been tested over a period of twenty years in a simulation by Dr John Price (mathematician and creator of the CI software). At the beginning of each year, any businesses that passed his stringent filters have been hypothetically purchased and then sold at the end of the same year. This simulation exercise has returned over 19% per annum.

Financial Ratios

The key financial ratios shown in Figure 6 are the main criteria applied in the filter to highlight businesses performing well.

I understand there are a plethora of ratios, and no holy grail, and I also concede each ratio can mean different things for different businesses, depending on the industry in which they operate. No single ratio will tell an investor all they need to know about a business. Some businesses require significant physical assets to operate, such as a mining business, whereas the assets of a software business are primarily its intellectual property (IP). Regardless of the industry, a combination of key ratios will contribute to building a financial picture of any business.

The ratios used in the filter within CI were selected by Dr John Price to provide the most essential information with proven validity. Step 1 of the CI methodology, the filtering process, identifies financially sound businesses, and the CI application adds a level of simplification to achieve this. Charlie Munger likes to invert so, to follow his principle, we can use the filter as an elimination tool to discard potential Capital Killers™ rather than searching for good businesses. In other words, trying to win by not losing.

The ratios to follow provide more information on the business's solvency, operating performance, debt leverage, and profitability. A fuller understanding of the business can be gained by becoming familiar with these ratios.

Earnings and sales per share

Over the previous five years, the earnings and sales should have ideally been steadily growing at over 3% (inflation) per annum. If not, we could simply leave our money in the bank.

Return on equity

How well is management working their asset base to make money for the business? This is reflected by the return on equity which should be greater than 10% over the past five years. We can only make as much as the business is making over the long term, so should we require a 10% return on our capital, the business needs to be making at least that.

Debt to equity

Taking on too much debt can be the catalyst to destroying a business, so the business should ideally show less than 50% debt to its equity.

Supporting Ratios

Current ratio

Commonly called the asset test ratio, this ratio shows the value of current assets versus the current liabilities of the business. Current means within 12 months.

Quick ratio

Similar to the Current ratio, but the stock/inventory element is removed from the current assets. The reason is that stock and inventory would be sold at, or even below, cost value should a business be liquidated.

Return on capital

Similar to the Return on Equity; however, this ratio is impacted by long-term debt commitments.

Interest cover

Shows how well the business can meet the interest payments on its debt commitments. We would become concerned about the viability of the business with an interest cover below five.

Net profit margin

The earnings that result from sales made by the business.

Types of Businesses

There are primarily three types of businesses—services, manufacturing, and merchandising (retailing).

Ideally, each business presents its set of accounts in accordance with the requirements and standards of International Financial Reporting Standards (IFRS) in Australia and Generally Accepted Accounting Principles

(GAAP) in America. However, bear in mind that the results may be presented in a manner that makes management and/or the business look good, which could improve the saleability or 'investability' of that business. In a move to improve transparency, the Australian Accounting Standards Board has recently introduced their AASB16 ruling which requires businesses to declare future lease obligations as a liability.

The detailed analyses of businesses can be both overwhelming and time-consuming. By scanning and filtering with the key financial ratios within CI, we can quickly access a shortlist of businesses worthy of more thorough research.

Why do Investors need Ratios?

Ratios provide an insight into a business and reveal a business's liquidity, operational efficiency, and profitability for the benefit of investors. These are the foundations of fundamental analysis.

In addition, ratio analysis assists investors in determining how well-managed a business is by substantiating the figures in the financial statements. Assessing ratios over a five-year period reveals whether a business is growing or deteriorating.

To draw an analogy, I monitor my flight instruments when flying a helicopter. Each instrument provides key information towards building an overall picture of how well the engine is operating and whether it is wise to continue flying or not.

Ratios are also useful for comparing businesses of any size within the same industry. For example, comparisons can be made between a large business such as CSL® (with a market cap of $143b) and a smaller peer such as Clinuvel® (market cap of $1b).

We observe trends over a longer period to avoid undue focus on short-term volatility. Any anomalies noticed should still be investigated as they may relate to such items as one-off write-downs or acquisitions.

The key components with benchmarks are:

Return on Capital (ROC)	Earnings ÷ (Equity + long-term debt) Greater than 10%
Return on Equity (ROE)	Earnings ÷ Equity (Assets – liabilities) [Book value] Greater than 10%
Debt to Equity (DEq)	Total debt ÷ Net Assets Less than 50%
Current Ratio (CR)	Current Assets ÷ Current Liabilities Greater than 1.25
Quick Ratio (QR)	(Current Assets – Inventory (Stock)) ÷ Current Liabilities Greater than 0.75
Interest Cover (IC)	Earnings ÷ Expenses (Interest related) Greater than 5
Market Capitalisation (MCap)	Number of shares X Share price Greater than A$100m
Net Profit Margin (NPM)	Earnings ÷ Sales Greater than 1% but determined by business model
Payout Ratio (PO)	Dividends ÷ Earnings Greater than 40%
Earnings per share (EPS)	Earnings ÷ Number of shares Growing faster than inflation—approx. 3%

Sales per share (SPS)	Revenue ÷ Number of shares Growing faster than inflation—approx. 3%
Price Earnings ratio (PE)	Price ÷ Earnings
Price earnings growth (PEG)	PE ÷ Earnings growth Less than 1

Table 2—Key components for Step 1

> The filter within CI applies the criteria to produce a manageable list of approximately 60 profitable businesses, with little or no debt, and a clear indication earnings will continue to grow.

Let's look in more detail at the ratios from Step 1:

Sales per Share (SPS)

> Sales per share = Sales ÷ Number of shares

A business must sell a product or service to make money. Sales then become the bedrock for earnings. The CI methodology advocates buying shares in businesses with consistent earnings and sales growth (ideally faster than inflation or at least at the current interest rate) and a positive outlook. Businesses worth considering should demonstrate a proven track record of growing sales and earnings.

While nobody knows for certain what the future will bring, we can begin by taking confidence from a positive historical performance. Then, to determine the future prospects of a business, we could assess their competition and how close they are to market saturation themselves. For example, most SUVs are fitted with ARB's vehicle accessories—what is their level of market domination, and is there still room for growth? What additional resources will be required?

Technology companies can often be scaled up to support new customers at relatively marginal cost and by utilising existing resources. As a result, there can be a huge increase in sales with little addition to expenses—any extra profit goes 'straight to their bottom line'. Should we find that sales are growing slower than earnings, it would be worthwhile to determine whether the business has increased the prices of their products/services, or undertaken some cost-cutting or improved margins, as this could become unsustainable in the longer term.

What we like to see is sales growing at a similar rate, or even faster, than earnings (see Figure 7). Sales growth is by far the most crucial factor in growing earnings. Take note of the consistency of this trend in the sales per share figures or chart. To achieve a growth in sales, a business can either expand its customer base, make an acquisition, or introduce new products or services. Another method is to raise product/service prices to increase net profit margins. However, this introduces a risk of driving customers away or encouraging lower-pricing competitors into the market.

Sales per share provides a more accurate figure than total sales, the reason being that a significant change in the SPS figure could more readily highlight a capital raising or share buyback.

To illustrate, if a business with one million shares made $10 million in sales, the sales equate to $10 per share. If the business buys back 10% of its shares, the shares on offer are reduced to 900,000, and the value per share increases to $11.11.

The workings are shown in Table 3.

	Total sales	Number of shares	Sales per share	Calculations
Before buyback	$10m	1m	$10	$10m ÷ 1m = $10
Buyback 10%		900,000		
After buyback	$10m	900,000	$11.11	$10m ÷ 900,000 = $11.11

Table 3—Buybacks

Bear in mind, a buyback may make the EPS of a business higher too as it will be 10% less diluted. The sales per share may grow from $10 per share to $11.11 per share; however, there is an associated cost to the business in purchasing back the 100,000 shares.

At this stage, it is helpful to start thinking about what the business sells (product or service) and ask yourself:

- Why would someone buy this product or use the service?
- Do its competitors sell a similar product or service?
- Does the business have an edge?
- How can the business generate more sales going forward?

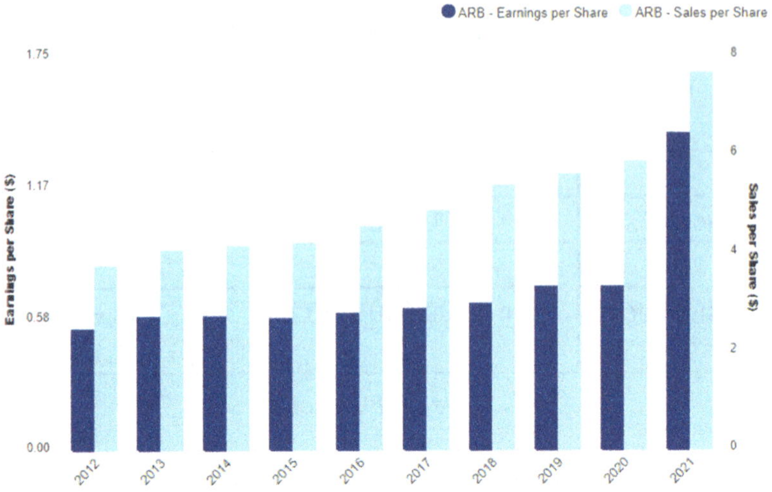

Figure 7—The correlated trend of the EPS and SPS for ARB

Earnings per Share (EPS)

Earnings per share = Earnings ÷ Number of shares

The profits (EPS) of a business are derived from its sales (SPS). Once again, the earnings per share provide a more accurate figure than total earnings.

Before we go any further, I'd like to mention that there are several 'earnings' figures. Please see Figure 8 below of how each 'earnings' figure is derived. (A magnified version of Figure 8 can be found on page 156 Figure 46).

PROFIT AND LOSS STATEMENT

Sales / Revenue	aka 'Top line'. Note: It is important to understand how the revenue is recognised i.e. upfront or over time.
- Cost of Goods	(COGS) Costs mainly for material & labour making the product or delivering the service. Also includes change in inventory. Mainly direct costs and some overhead allocation
= Gross Profit	aka Gross Income
- Expenses	S,G & A' (Selling, General & Adminstration) expenses. Money spent to develop, sell or account for the product and manage the making and selling process. Overheads which are incurred with the running of the business that cannot be directly related to the cost of making or purchasing the things the business sells
= Earnings before Tax, Interest, Depreciation and Amortisation	(EBITDA) Operating income
- Depreciation and amortisation expense	
= Earnings Before Income Tax and Interest	(EBIT)
- Interest expense	
= Earnings before Tax	EBT aka PBT (Profit before Tax)
- Income tax expense	
= Net Profit after Tax	(NPAT) Reported or Statutory or Operating earnings
- / + Abnormal or Extraordinary items	i.e. Acquistion costs, write offs or downs
= Net Profit After Tax and Abnormals	(NPAT) aka 'Bottom line', Normalised or Underlying

Basic earnings = earnings / o/s equity shares of the company (outstanding common shares)
Diluted earnings = earnings / all shares (options etc) Present a clearer picture of EPS
Statutory profit = the earnings that standard accounting practices require a company to report on its income statement
Statutory figures are those presented by the company in their formal company reports. They include all items that affect the earnings and are audited

Figure 8—Key components of a profit and loss statement showing the various earning figures

Throughout the book, any reference to earnings will refer to the 'Underlying' earnings figure.

ARB's clear and simple profit and loss statement can be seen below. Their format is even simpler than the standard format in Figure 8 in that COGS have not been separated but incorporated into the 'expenses' section.

PROFIT AND LOSS STATEMENT	2021 $m
Sales revenue	623
Other income	3
Total revenue and other income	**626**
Materials and consumables used	(279)
Employee expenses	(129)
Government wage subsidies	10
Depreciation and amortisation expense	(24)
Advertising expenses	(6)
Distribution expenses	(14)
Finance expenses	(2)
Occupancy expenses	(14)
Maintenance expenses	(5)
Other expenses	(13)
Profit before income tax expenses	**150**
Income tax expenses	(37)
Profit attributable to members of the parent entity	**113**
Basic & Diluted Earnings per share (cents)	**140.0**

Figure 9—ARB's profit and loss statement

Interestingly, of the 2,288 businesses currently trading on the ASX, less than half are actually profitable. Why would you even consider investing in an unprofitable business? The media headlines make compelling reading by highlighting businesses with a rising share price while often ignoring the fact that they make no profit. One example of this is Afterpay.

In the long term, the share price tends to follow earnings, which is why Teaminvest members ignore daily share price fluctuations and focus entirely on earnings and sales.

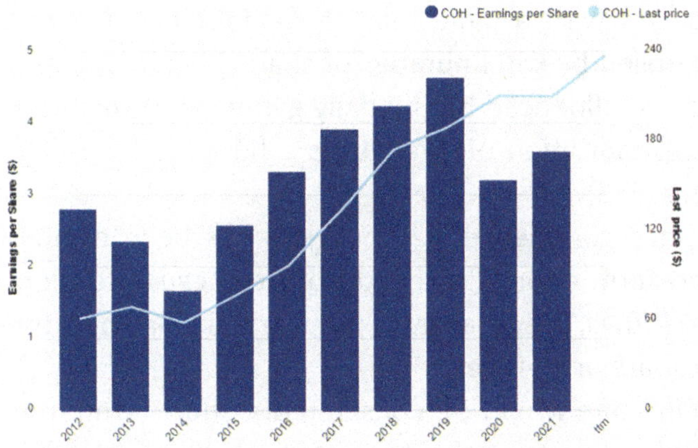

Figure 10—Price following earnings for Cochlear®[18]

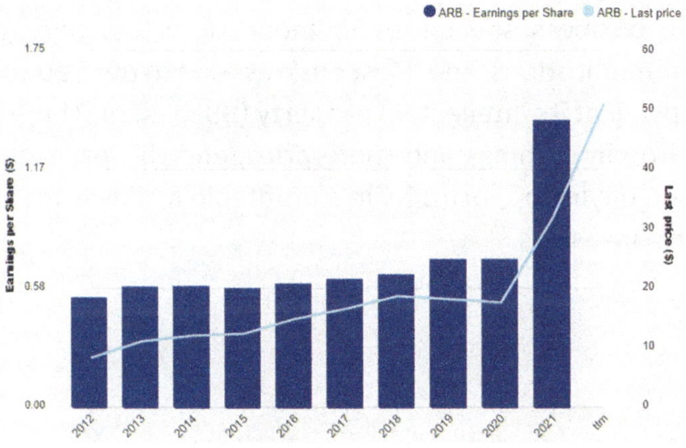

Figure 11—Price following earnings for ARB[19]

Ideally, we want the earnings per share to be growing steadily each year, and if they are not, we would do well to investigate the reasons why. For example, there may be the cost of an acquisition or an expansion of the existing business. In addition, there could be occasional one-offs, such as a write-down of intangible assets or the sale of a building, which can impact results in any given year.

Some investors think there is less risk investing in a business with a large market capitalisation (share price multiplied by total number of shares). However, as share price is influenced by the daily gyrations of the market, a better indication of strength is a business's earnings per share (EPS).

Once confidence in a business has been established, short-term anomalies need not be a cause for concern. Sometimes, they may even provide a buying opportunity if the share price falters.

One-offs would be considered a short-term anomaly. Specific details of the one-off cost can be found in the business's annual report under notes associated with the financials. Codan® provides us with an example. The business specialises in metal detectors and radio communications, and it lost business due to the fraudulent copying of its intellectual property (IP) in 2014. There was a drop in earnings and share price, and this presented a good buying opportunity in a profitable business for long-term investors.[20]

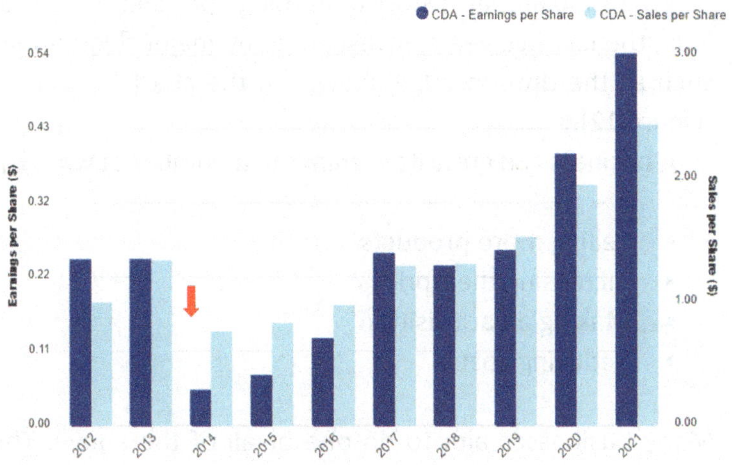

Figure 12—EPS and SPS for Codan[21]

Underlying vs statutory earnings

Underlying (sometimes called normalised) earnings is an oft-used measure to show how much a business normally makes each year. If a business has had a one-off cost or an abnormal expense such as an acquisition, this cost may not be reflected in underlying earnings. When a business states profits have grown, we might legitimately wonder which of the five profit figures they are referring to. Figure 8 shows all the iterations of the earnings (profit).

By contrast, a statutory or reported profit includes any one-offs. If there is a significant difference between statutory and underlying earnings per share, be sure to investigate the reason why: perhaps an acquisition or a sale of part of the business.

As an individual, a profit or loss is only reflected in our returns once it has been 'realised'. By contrast, a company may reflect the current value of any shareholdings they own, in another public listed company, although they remain unrealised.

When looking at historical earnings per share, over at least the last five years, investigate any major fluctuations such as the drop in 2014 shown on the chart for Codan. (Figure 12).

A business can grow its earnings in a number of ways by:

- Selling more products
- Increasing their prices
- Making an acquisition
- Reducing costs.

Many businesses aim to do one or all of the above. The three major financial statements, produced at financial year-end, will assist in determining which strategies are being applied.

We love to find businesses whose earnings are growing, although we need to be satisfied that the growth is sustainable and realistic. A reasonable growth rate for earnings in a well-established business is around 10% per annum. A higher growth rate of earnings is more likely found in recently listed businesses that are starting from a lower base.

Earnings will naturally slow in established businesses as their products or services reach critical mass.

Peer comparison can be a particularly useful exercise in assessing what earnings are reasonable. If we are considering buying Resmed®, for instance, we could compare its earnings per share with Fisher & Paykel® as both are in the healthcare industry and sell related products.

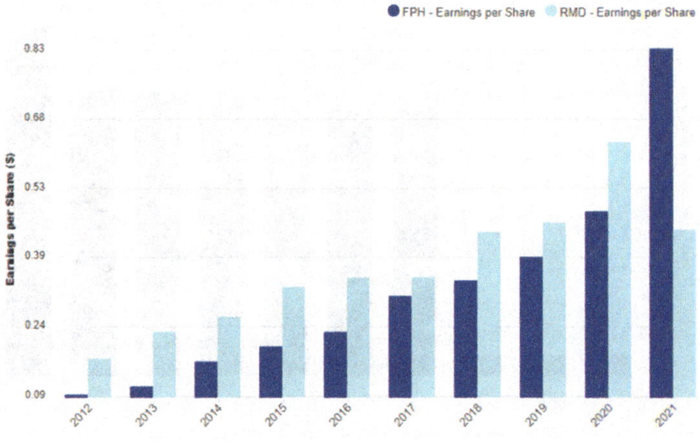

Figure 13—EPS for Fisher & Paykel versus Resmed[22]

Business needs more capital

When a business needs to expand, it could draw on retained earnings, take on debt or initiate a capital raising (by issuing more shares). While capital raisings dilute the value of existing shares, the good news is the business has more capital to deploy. Understanding the reason behind the decision is key.

The next graph shows the shares on issue for ARB. It raised capital to build a manufacturing facility in Thailand in 2015. Prior to the expansion, it had 72.5 million shares on offer. The capital raising expanded this by a further 6.7 million shares which diluted its earnings per share by 9.24%.

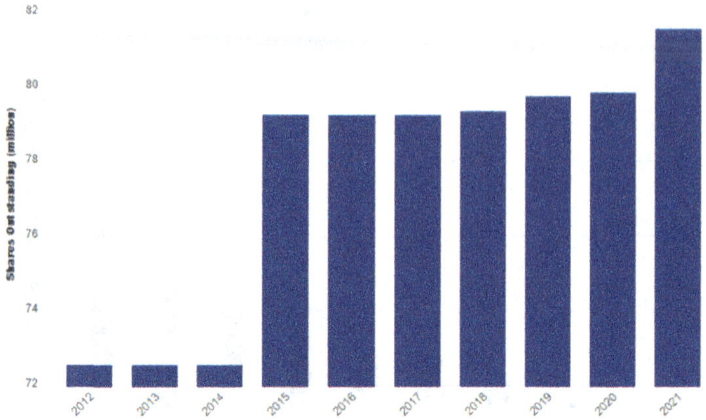

Figure 14—Shares outstanding: ARB[23]

The opposite scenario is a buyback of shares which reduces the total number of shares on issue and increases the value of each individual share. This has occurred progressively over the years with CSL.

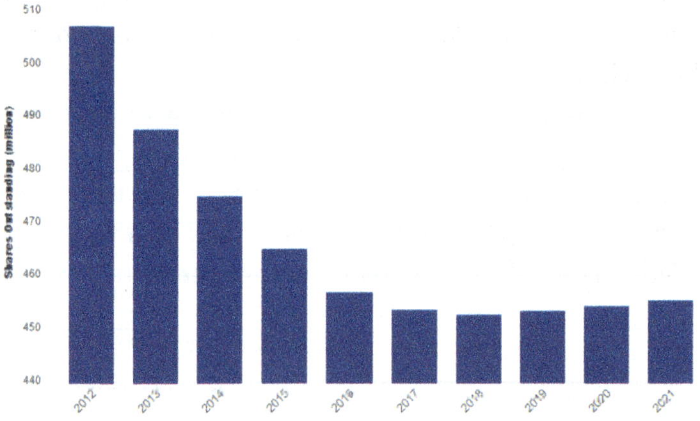

Figure 15—Shares outstanding: CSL[24]

Earnings growth

When a business first starts to operate, there is potential to achieve an earnings growth above 20%. However, as a fast grower, it's likely to reach market saturation sooner, bearing in mind Australia's comparatively modest population of 25 million.

To continue their positive growth rate, Australian businesses are often forced to expand abroad, requiring proficiency in different business cultures. The populations of China and India are over a billion people each, with the USA over 331 million. Some remarkably successful examples of international expansion are CSL and Cochlear, but there are many unsuccessful examples, such as the foray of the banks into Asia (ANZ) and into the UK and USA (NAB). It's easier for a business to grow annual sales from $1 to $10 million than from $100 to $200 million.

We can, therefore, deduce that higher growth is more often found in newer businesses with good prospects. These businesses are often smaller, nimbler, and are frequently run by their founders. Although they are viewed positively, we should be particularly mindful of their vulnerability compared to larger, more established competitors.

Small businesses have the potential to grow faster than larger ones. There are exceptions, however, with some large businesses defying their size to find ways to expand their earnings, as has been demonstrated by CSL.

As Lynch says, 'You should look at a growth company and say I don't want to buy it when they are in the first innings. I want to buy it when they are in the second or third innings. They have got the right formula, they got lots of room to go.'[25]

Look out for anomalies in the trends of a business's sales and earnings over time (at least five years). The ideal trend is a consistent, steady increase. During the GFC, when share prices dropped significantly, the earnings of great businesses such as Technology One® (TNE) and ARB showed negligible changes. At Teaminvest, we consider such events to be excellent opportunities to buy shares in great businesses at bargain prices.

Figure 16—EPS and share price for TNE[27]

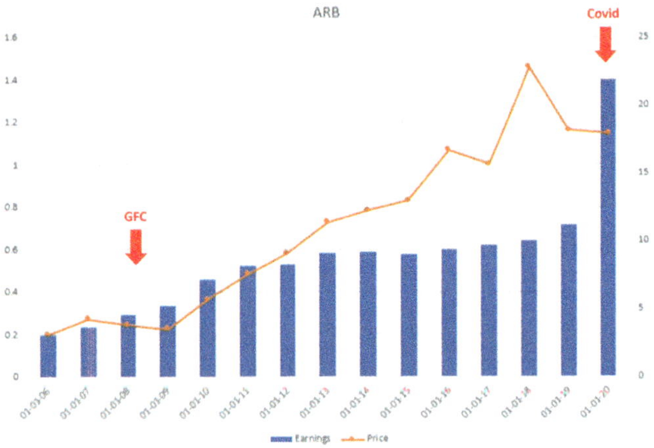

Figure 17—EPS and share price for ARB[26]

The management of a business has various options as to how it allocates its surplus earnings. Most businesses retain a sizeable portion of their earnings to facilitate their growth, either by expanding organically or by acquiring other businesses. Or management could elect to buy back shares or pay a shareholder dividend. While a generous dividend is certainly appealing to most investors, it should not be to the detriment of business growth.

Net Profit Margin (NPM)

Net profit margin = (Earnings ÷ Sales) x 100

NPM shows what portion of profit comes from sales. The NPM should be growing or, at the very least, be consistent over at least five years. A business with a larger net profit margin has more wriggle room and a wider safety net as enjoyed by TNE shown in the chart below.

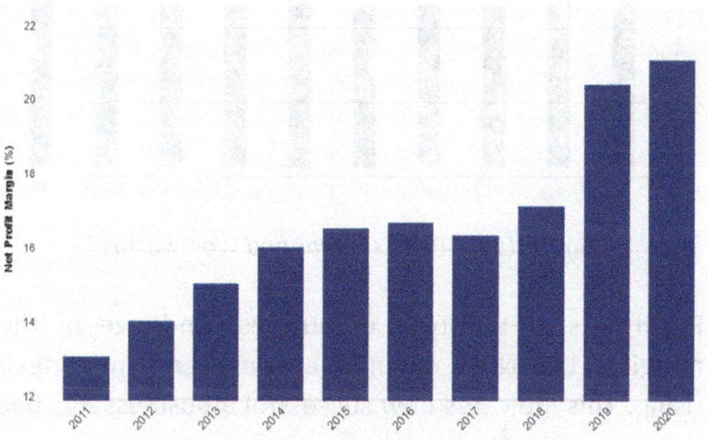

Figure 18—NPM for TNE[28]

It is worth noting that just because a business has low margins does not make it a poor business. Several well-known businesses outperform despite low margins, for instance, Amazon®. In Australia, Data#3® is a technology solutions business with a long history of profitability, despite low margins of just over 1%.

Some businesses achieve a high sales volume and low prices (for example, Woolworths®—average NPM 4%) while others have low sales volumes and high prices (for example, Cochlear—average NPM 15%). Consider the type of business and determine where it sits on the NPM scale, preferably at one end or the other, not in the middle.

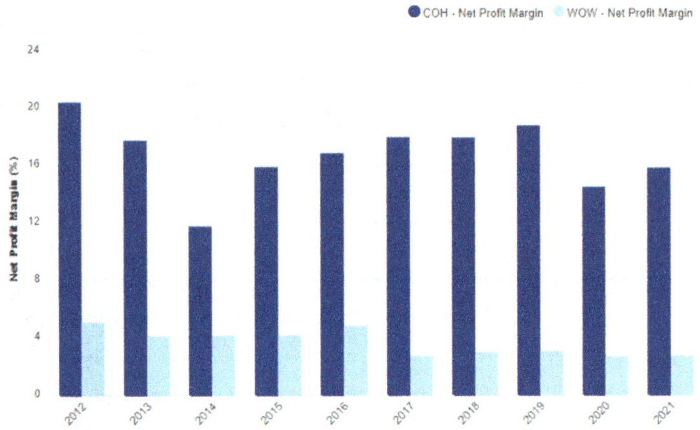

Figure 19—NPM: Cochlear and Woolworths[29]

Regardless of the type of business and size of their margins, the NPM should be consistent and, ideally, rising. This indicates how successful a business has been in managing costs.

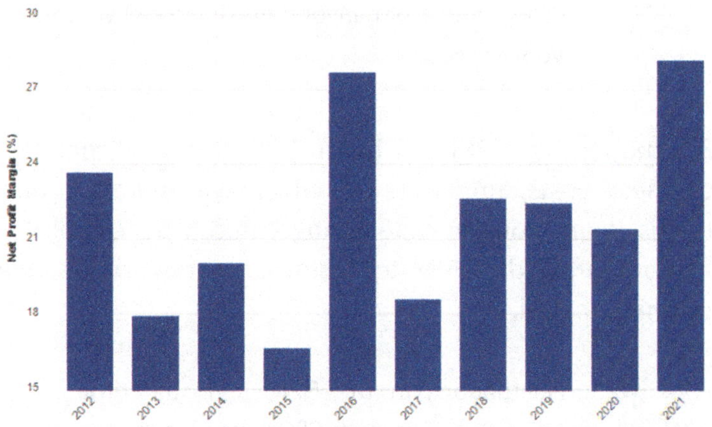

Figure 20—NPM for BHP[30]

A business with an erratic NPM is BHP, due in part to its reliance on commodity prices. Mining businesses are particularly capital-intensive and can only be as successful as the quality and quantity of their mines. They are constantly searching for new mines and may need to commit much of their earnings into finding, establishing, and maintaining the next mine.

At Teaminvest, we consider BHP to be a 'price-taker'. That is, it can only sell its products for the prevailing price of the commodity, such as iron ore. Personally, I lean towards businesses that are *price-makers*, such as Cochlear, a hearing aid manufacturer with great control over its product prices.

Tip

'Ticket clippers' are so-called as they rely on the volume of sales with minimal additional costs to make these sales. An example: SYM Holdings Limited has an established infrastructure in voice and data communications, and it continues to collect fees from anyone making a call via their VoIP service.

Fluctuations in NPM can be an indicator of a change in business costs, up or down, which will impact profits. If this is an industry-wide change, it can be established by comparing the NPM to business peers with a similar business model.

Tip

Fluctuations in the NPM can sometimes be attributed to a new CEO being appointed and wanting to 'clear the decks'—that is, reduce expenditure or perhaps write off the debt.

Return on Equity and Return on Capital (ROE/ROC)

Return on Equity (ROE) = (Earnings ÷ Equity) x 100

Return on equity (ROE) can best be described by referring to ARB, whose assets are the vehicle accessories that they manufacture. The business incurs expenses and sometimes debt (liabilities) to produce and market these assets. ARB ships the finished products around Australia and worldwide and is paid for the products (earnings).

So, for investors to earn at least 10% on their investments in the business, the business must itself be making at least 10% ROE. The measure reveals how hard the management is working its equity (assets less liabilities) to deliver a profit for the business and its shareholders. Compare ROE between competitors in the same industry, as they should be similar.

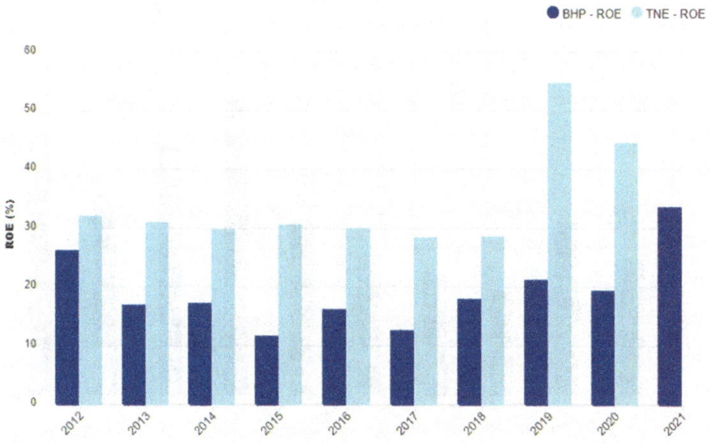

Figure 21—ROE: BHP and TNE[31]

It is important to be aware of the different business models between industries—many IT businesses hold minimal assets compared to asset-heavy resources businesses. The *equity* in the ROE figure is assets less liabilities, therefore, based on the ROE formula, a business with fewer assets (denominator) has a higher ROE.[32]

Return on Capital (ROC) = ((Earnings ÷ (Equity + Debt))) x 100

If a business has no debt, the ROE equals ROC, which in turn measures how well the business is functioning with all its resources at hand (equity plus debt). Consider the ROE in conjunction with the ROC to avoid being lured solely by a higher ROE.

Domino's Pizza® has steadily taken on more and more debt for overseas expansions over a 10-year period. This would contribute to its significant increase in debt to equity, from 14% in 2010 to over 375% in 2020. As a result, it has high ROE but declining ROC.[33]

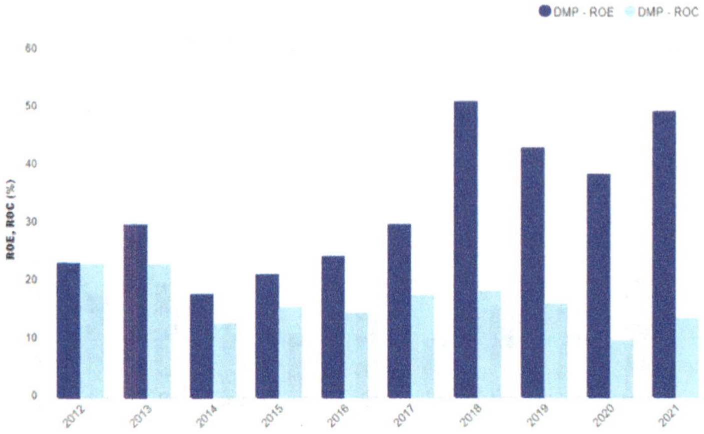

Figure 22—ROE and ROC for Domino's Pizza (DMP)[34]

Investors will find a high ROE (above 10%) attractive, and the potential increase in investments could drive up the share price. Financial ratios normally relate to one of the three major reports. The benefit of considering the ROE and ROC ratios together is they span two reports, the balance sheet (equity) and the profit and loss statement (earnings), and provide a good overview of a business's financial position.

Intangible assets

Goodwill is an example of an intangible asset, which can be ascribed a monetary value although it cannot be *seen*. When one business acquires another, there is often some form of goodwill, such as a database of clientele in an established hairdressing business, which will then be reflected as an intangible asset in the balance sheet. Another example of intangibles could be brand or intellectual property (IP). However, the values placed on any intangible assets can be subjective.

When a business is under pressure, its intangibles may be viewed less favourably by investors. Should the intangibles subsequently be written off, there will be a negative impact to earnings. Serial acquirers would be faced with the handling of intangible assets on a more frequent basis.

Price/Earnings (PE)

PE = Share Price ÷ Earnings

The PE is a measure used to relate a business's earnings to its share price. As a general rule, anything around 17, being the average market PE, is considered fair value. Fair value is what the market is prepared to pay based on the business's earnings. Assuming the fundamentals are sound, a lower-than-average PE could provide a buying opportunity.

A higher PE, therefore, suggests it may be deemed too expensive so only consider a purchase if you are greatly confident that earnings will grow over time.

For example, if a business has a share price of $20 and earnings per share of $1, then its PE becomes 20 (that is, $20 ÷ 1). It will therefore take twenty years of earnings (assuming no growth) to repay an investor's capital outlay at the current share price.

Let's look at the data taken from CI for ARB®:

	Jun-11	Jun-12	Jun-13	Jun-14	Jun-15	Jun-16	Jun-17	Jun-18	Jun-19	Jun-20	Jun-21
P/E High	16.30	18.20	23.60	23.60	25.10	28.40	29.80	37.20	32.50	28.80	34.00
P/E Low	10.70	12.50	15.30	17.80	18.10	20.90	23.00	23.30	20.30	14.50	17.60
Price High	8.49	9.65	13.82	13.88	14.49	17.00	18.50	23.94	23.32	20.64	47.58
Price Low	5.60	6.65	8.93	10.46	10.49	12.52	14.28	14.99	14.55	10.40	17.68

Table 4—ARB's PEs and Prices

In table 4, if we were to compare the June 2013 low price of \$8.93 to the June 2020 low price of \$10.40, we see a dollar value increase. However, by comparing the June 2013 PE (15.3) to the June 2020 PE (14.5), we notice a decrease. This indicates the low price in June 2020 presented a better buying opportunity. To clarify, think about a business with a share price of \$10, and an earnings per share of \$1—hence a PE of 10. Several years later, the earnings per share has grown to \$4 and the share price to \$20 suggesting you may have missed the boat. But the PE of 5 offers a far better value and avoids the risk of anchoring on price, making it easier to add to existing holdings down the track.

To measure if the PE is too high, we could compare it to the growth of earnings, called the PEG.

PEG = PE ÷ Earnings growth

If the PEG is around 1, it is considered fair value. With a PE of 20 and a 20% growth of earnings, the resulting PEG is 1.

PEG = 20 (PE) ÷ 20 (Earnings growth) = 1

Using the same formula, if we assume an earnings growth of 10%, the PEG would be 2 (20 ÷ 10) which suggests that the shares may be too expensive to purchase at this time. For more detail on this subject, read the chapter 'PEG and Friends' in *The Conscious Investor*® book.[11]

The PE of fairly priced businesses is about equal to the expected annual growth rate over the next three to five years. If the PE is substantially higher than the growth rate, the business is considered expensive, and a substantially lower PE indicates that it's well-priced.

When assessing a business for potential investment, a peer comparison of the PE and growth rate is useful. A low PE and high growth rate are positive indicators.

Tip

Businesses with a feel-good factor and deep moats, such as the excellent intellectual property of Cochlear and CSL, will generally have consistently high PEs.

Debt to Equity (D/E)

Debt to Equity = (Debt ÷ Equity) x 100

Almost all businesses incur debt. A business normally commits its total equity and long-term debt in order to grow. Ideally, we invest in businesses with less than 50% debt to equity and certainly no more than 70%. When interest rates rise, additional pressure is placed on businesses to meet their debt obligations, and this can become detrimental to their growth in earnings.

The present COVID-19 pandemic has exacerbated the situation of businesses struggling to repay their debt due to their earnings being unexpectedly eroded. Virgin Australia®, a high-profile victim of the pandemic, found their revenues ceased almost overnight when the government imposed blanket travel lockdowns. Debt obligations of around $7b could not be met, which resulted in the restructure and takeover of the business.[35]

Let's explore when businesses are likely to incur debt and the impact that debt can have.

There are two approaches a business could take to expand. They could do so organically, by increasing their sales, or they could acquire other businesses to enhance their overall production. Both approaches require funds, so the business must spend what reserves they hold and/or obtain a bank loan and/or undertake a capital raising.

A reasonable level of debt is considered acceptable for any business, provided earnings continue to grow and repayment obligations can be met. Borrowed money is subject to interest payments and, when interest rates are low, it becomes more appealing for businesses to borrow despite the risk of over-extending themselves.

Rising interest rates also have the potential to spook customers, who may reduce their own spending, and investors could then choose cash investments over share market investments.

Both aspects could result in a business starting to show signs of distress, whereby peers could start to circle, hoping for a takeover opportunity. Should covenants then be breached, the banks could begin calling in loans which would have the potential to make the business operations unsustainable.

Adopt the following benchmarks as a safe guideline:

- Debt to equity ratio ideally below 50%
- Interest cover (earnings ÷ interest expenses) ideally above five times
- Debt to market capitalisation (MCap) ideally less than 10%.

The GFC of 2008/09 highlighted the impact high levels of debt can impose on some businesses. Babcock & Brown® and ABC Developmental Learning Centres did not survive, yet debt-free businesses such as Technology One and ARB survived and prospered.[36]

Capital raising is one of the strategies by which a cash poor business could raise additional funds. If a business with a market capitalisation of $100 million has a debt of $10 million, equating to 10%, a capital raising of just one new share to every ten shares held would clear that debt. This small capital raising is likely to be acceptable to investors, while a higher percentage would dilute the value of the shares more significantly and be less well received.

The surest way to fully understand a business's financial position is to read and study its annual and interim reports. In the balance sheet, the value of physical assets, plus cash held, should ideally be higher than the liabilities (including long- and short-term debt). A business with plenty of cash available could feasibly pay off its debt, make acquisitions, or expand organically by opening more stores. As a rule of thumb, an ideal business has no debt and enough cash on hand to cover current liabilities.

A side note on debt: Industries, such as retailers, may have long-term rental commitments on their premises. The future commitments of rent historically appeared as a footnote in the business financials (off the balance sheet). However, a recent ruling has changed this, and businesses must now show future rent commitments as a liability in the balance sheet. Although the debt has no immediate material impact on the health of the business, it provides investors with a more accurate view of the business's future obligations.

Tip

I refer to the accounting notes in a business's annual report and compare several years for any glaring differences between major items which require further investigation. Before the advent of the internet, investment professionals enjoyed a huge advantage over retail investors with access to quicker in-depth market and business financial information. Nowadays, the same information is freely available for everyone to access for their investing research.

Cash Flow

There is an apt saying: 'Price is vanity, profit is sanity, and cash is reality'. With cash reporting, it is more difficult for businesses to apply creative accounting, and their performance is far more transparent. That said, be mindful of how a business handles its cash. For instance, Woolworths receives cash immediately from its customers, yet may only be required to pay its supplier commitments at a later date. Therefore, it's quite easy to misconstrue their financial position between reporting periods.

Tip

Operating cash flow (cash on hand to operate the business) less cash outgoings (investing activities) results in free cash flow. Compare the result to historical levels of cash flow to pick up any trends. Decreasing cash flow is a cause for concern.

CASHFLOW STATEMENT	2021 $m
Cash Flows From Operating Activities	
Receipts from customers	651
Payments to suppliers and employees	-516
Interest received	0.1
Finance costs	(2)
Income tax paid	-30
Net cash provided by Operating activities	**103**
Cash Flows From Investing Activities	
Payments for property, plant and equipment	-33
Payments for development costs	-3
Payments for intangible software assets	-0.7
Proceeds from sales of property, plant & equipment	0.8
Payments for business acquisition	-15
Net cash used in Investing activities	**(51)**
Cash Flows From Financing Activities	
Dividends paid	
Payments for lease liabilities	-0.5
Proceeds from borrowings	-5
Repayment of borrowings	**-3**
Net cash used in Financing activities	**(9)**
Foreign exchange differences	0.4
Net increase / (decrease) in cash held	**43**
Cash at the beginning of the financial year	42
Cash at the end of the financial year	85

Figure 23—ARB's cash flow statement

Most businesses do not utilise much physical cash in their day-to-day operations and, instead, provide payment terms for their customers, sometimes as far out as ninety days. Likewise, when paying its suppliers, the business may be granted payment terms.

The cash flow statement is different from the profit and loss statement which includes inflows and outflows recorded on credit.

A business will be in a better position the more cash it holds, and the cash flow statement provides a transparent and essential assessment, indicating how well it can meet its future expenses.

I learned just how critical cash is to a fast-growing business from the wonderful book *Shoe Dog*, by the founder of Nike, Phil Knight. In its first month of production, Nike sold almost all their entire stock of shoes and, notwithstanding the income made from those sales, the expectation of massive demand the following month required advance funding in order to produce enough stock. As the demand for shoes continued to grow apace, the banks became reticent to advance more credit to Nike as the cash outflows to make shoes preceded the inflows from shoe sales. This did not provide sufficient security in the banking world.[37]

Payout Ratio (Dividends)

Payout ratio = (Dividends ÷ Earnings) x 100

The portion of earnings paid out as dividends is called the payout ratio. It is a preferable measure to dividend yield which is based on the fluctuating share price and can, therefore, be deceiving.

For example, business XYZ has a dividend yield of 5% which appears attractive. The share price is currently $5, which means the dividend equates to 25c per share. If the share price then halves, the yield becomes 10%. Is the business now even more attractive? No, as the overall return (capital growth plus dividends) has been significantly reduced. This is often called a *value trap*.

Many investors rely on dividends to supplement their income and perceive dividends as a benefit when selecting an investment. However, it's important to realise that some businesses incur debt to pay a dividend in order to appease their shareholders, risking the impact of their increased debt obligations.

The equivalent of the dividend distribution may be better applied to reducing existing debt and/or growing the business. Businesses that decide against dividend payments may be viewed negatively by income-seeking investors, the media, and fund managers. However, such a decision is sometimes reflective of sensible, forward-thinking management. Ideally, search for great businesses before checking their dividend payout—not the other way around.

In Australia, investors may benefit from dividends with franking credits, which can provide an appealing tax benefit. This results in a relatively less volatile share market than the USA, where franking credits do not apply and capital gains benefit from tax breaks rather than dividends.

Tip

A useful exercise is to record the value of each dividend distribution, including franking credits, against your capital outlay on each shareholding. There's a break-even point when the dividend income has covered the initial cost of the holding and all future gains become unencumbered profit.

Refer to the illustration in the table below which can be used as a template.

Code	Capital invested	Dividend year	Dividend paid
XYZ	$20,000	2016	$800
		2017	$890
		2018	$980
		2019	$1,050
= $4,960 / $20,000		2020	$1,240
24.8%			**$4,960**

Table 5—Total annual dividend as % of outlay

Focusing on long-term income rather than the share price of the stock provides a good motivation to remain a long-term investor.

As business earnings increase, the dividend income would also increase, despite the payout ratio remaining unchanged. Assume a business has a payout ratio of 50%. As the earnings rise each year (say, by 10%), the 50% payout ratio will then be calculated on the higher earnings figure.

Although Technology One's average payout ratio over ten years is 69.5%, the dollar value of the dividend has grown each year in line with the earnings.

Figure 24—Earnings and dividends of TNE[38]

Whilst we like our dividend income to keep growing, we must applaud a prudent business retaining funds to pay off debt, grow the business, or take an opportunity to make an acquisition.

Many investors, especially if they are retired, are naturally drawn to good dividend-payers at the expense of capital growth. However, an element of capital growth higher than inflation ensures their capital is not eroding. I therefore propose striving to build a portfolio containing investments that provide some rate of capital growth, as well as paying a dividend, and allowing the magic of compounding to work.

Compound interest is said to be the eighth wonder of the world. Albert Einstein was apparently asked, 'What do you consider to be man's greatest invention?' He is reported to have replied, 'Compound interest.'[39]

Chapter Summary

We have now discussed all the key financial ratios used to filter out exceptional businesses based on their metrics. This process allows the investor to focus their time and effort on a small group of businesses, rather than the entire ASX. The group of approximately 60 quality businesses will feature sound financials, such as growing earnings and sales, low debt levels, and consistent returns on equity. The probability is that they will continue to thrive in the future, particularly if they pass step 2 in the next chapter. So, fasten your seatbelt!

Activity: From the list of businesses derived from the filter results, sort them into sectors and determine which business sectors fall within your circle of competence. You may already have an understanding of how they may operate and the challenges they would face. Can you foresee that any of these businesses may become redundant, phased out, or superseded by newer technology, products, or processes in the next ten years? The qualitative filtering to follow will reduce your list further to a core group of sound companies in which you might consider investing.

Notes

Chapter 5
Step 2—The Qualitative Analysis of a Business

Qualitative research delves into areas such as the quality, commitment, and performance of management, the business model being employed, the prospects of the industry, and the benefits and challenges that affect businesses within it. As every person has unique business and life experiences, this research may result in different outcomes for each potential investor.

Quality over Quantity

The aim at Teaminvest is to promote concentrated value investing, with a goal to hold a portfolio of approximately 15–20 share investments, ideally spread across several sectors. It's important to be aware that the greater the number of holdings, the closer the results will match the index and, consequently, the harder it becomes to outperform. Therefore, it makes sense to spend more time and effort on analysing and purchasing fewer, high-quality businesses. Initially, we could identify approximately 25 businesses that we are interested in and know something about, or have some knowledge of the sector in which they reside.

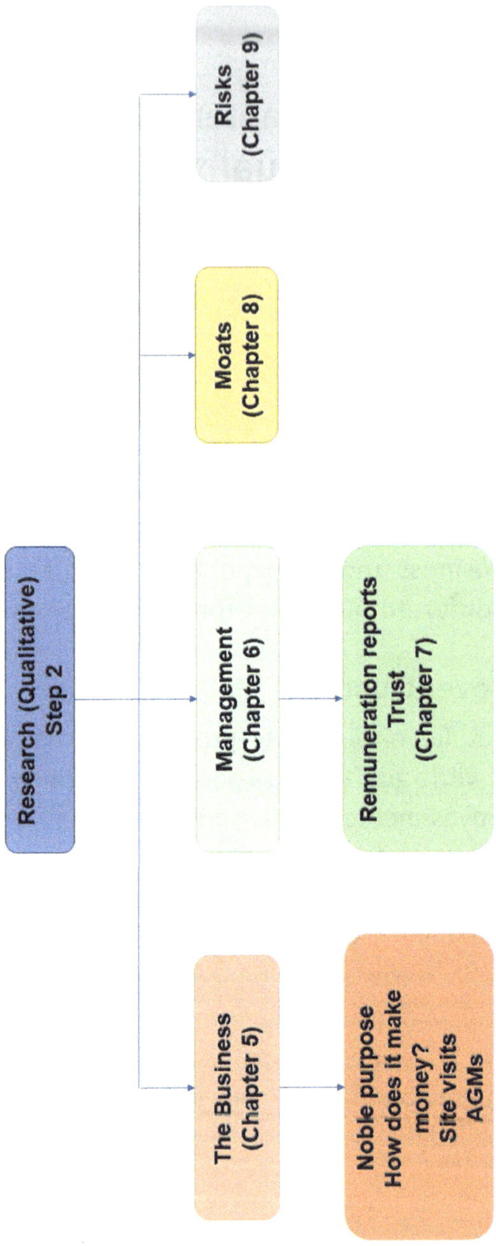

Figure 25—Step 2: Research. Key components

Consider businesses making products and services that are resilient and don't change over time. We may conclude that predictable products/services equate to predictable profits. It's interesting to mention here that Warren Buffett's largest holdings are in Apple®, Coca-Cola®, American Express®, and Bank of America® which account for over 65% of his publicly listed portfolio.[40]

For a deeper understanding of the specific business cultures and operations, there is much to be gained by reading annual reports, attending annual general meetings, and taking the time to visit business premises wherever practical. After all, we only need to know a few very well.

Peter Lynch describes this as: 'If you're prepared to invest in a business, then you ought to be able to explain why, in simple language that a fifth-grader could understand, and quickly enough so the fifth-grader won't get bored.'[41]

The Key Components of the Business that Need to be Analysed

The first process is to consider some of these questions:

1. What type of business is it and what does it do?
2. How does it make money?
3. Is it capital intensive? (If so, expect a low ROE.)
4. What industry does it fall within? Is it a cyclical or steady industry?
5. Is this industry currently experiencing headwinds or tailwinds?
6. Look up its website to gain an impression of the business.
7. Can you foresee that the business will still be around in ten or more years? What is your gut feeling?

By way of an example, if we were to favour Cochlear as a potential investment, can we foresee any major changes to its business within ten years? Are there any significant threats to the business from competitors and what form might they take? For example, superior quality, product innovation, or perhaps technology disruption.

Working through the questions above, as they apply to Cochlear, relevant observations could be:

1. Manufacturer of hearing aids, sold to doctors with which they have strong relationships.
2. They provide vital connections for hearing-impaired people to the world around them.
3. The relatively low capital outlay in the medical industry.
4. The health sector is steady and generally not cyclical.
5. Tailwinds due to the ageing baby boomer market.
6. Founder mentality still in place although the founder is no longer present.
7. Proven reliability and longevity with an overall upward trend and sentiment. Some competition and product alternatives exist.

By employing a kind of helicopter view, we gain more of a gut feel for an individual business. As a result, we will become more intuitively aware of anomalies in the business financials when undertaking detailed research.

Components of the share market

For ease of reference, businesses are classified into sector/industry groups known as the Global Industry Classification Standard (GICS®). Businesses are classified by their primary industry, even in the instance where they may have spread across different sectors due to business expansions and adaptations to market conditions. Wesfarmers® is one example, having begun in the retail sector and then branching out into resources, namely coal.

The division of sectors and industries is illustrated below:

Sector	Industry Group
Energy	Energy Equipment & Services Oil, Gas & Consumable Fuels
Materials	Chemicals, Construction Materials, Containers & Packaging, Aluminium Diversified Metals & Mining Precious Metals & Minerals, Silver, Steel, Paper & Forest Products
Industrials	Capital Goods, Commercial & Professional Services Transportation
Consumer Discretionary	Automobiles & Components Consumer Durables & Apparel, Consumer Services, Media Retailing
Consumer Staples	Food & Staples Retailing, Food, Beverage & Tobacco, Household & Personal Products
Health Care	Health Care Equipment & Services Pharmaceuticals, Biotechnology & Life Sciences
Financials	Banks, Other Diversified Financial Services, Multi-Sector Holdings, Specialised Finance, Consumer Finance, Capital Markets Insurance

Information Technology	Software & Services Technology, Hardware & Equipment, Semiconductors & Semiconductors Equipment
Telecommunication Services	Diversified Telecommunication, Wireless Telecommunication Media & Entertainment
Utilities	Electric, Gas, Multi-Utilities, Water, Industrial Power & Renewable Electricity Producers
Real Estate	Equity Real Estate Investment Trusts (REITs), Real Estate Management & Development

Table 6—Sectors and industries of the ASX

Teaminvest adopts the bottom-up approach; that is, starting at the business level, then the industry, the sector, and finally the market as a whole. The three main sectors most affected by economic and market forces, making them cyclical, are materials (for example, a mining boom or bust), financials (for example, bull and bear markets) and consumer discretionary (for example, changes in the economy). Health, consumer staples, and utilities are steadier and, as such, considered to be defensive.

Noble purpose and the emotional impact on customers

Many businesses make money through the subtle yet highly appealing nature of their 'noble purpose'. It describes the emotional impact a business has on its customers and is different from a mission statement, which relates more to the organisation itself. For example, Cochlear's noble purpose is: 'Hear now. And always. Hearing connects us to our world. To small everyday wonders and to the people and experiences we love.'[42]

As Cochlear changes people's lives through its network of doctors and products, it evokes powerful emotions in its customers with these words.

The mission statement is more organisational: 'We help people hear and be heard. We empower people to connect with others and live a full life. We help transform the way people understand and treat hearing loss.'

Tip

I'd recommend watching an inspiring documentary on Graeme Clark, inventor of the cochlear hearing device—it's a story of perseverance and limitless belief in himself, despite having to bear some ridicule along the way.[43]

'In spite of the problems and criticisms, I just had to go on. A cochlear implant was their only hope of ever hearing.'

—Professor Graeme Clark

Behind most successful businesses is an impactful noble purpose and/or mission statement.

A ten-year growth study (Stengel) was undertaken on a global database of more than 50,000 brands and businesses were ranked by the degree to which they improved lives, transcending their products and services. The five fields of fundamental human values are:

- Eliciting joy
- Enabling connection
- Inspiring exploration
- Evoking pride
- Impacting society.[44]

An investment in the top 50 businesses, named the 'Stengel 50', would be 400 percent more profitable than an investment in the S&P 500 over the same 10-year period, a difference of 17.9% per annum.

According to this same study, 'Top performing brands are built on ideals and higher-order purposes that transcend products and services.'

These statements inspire an improvement in business sales and ultimately, earnings. It stands to reason we instinctively align with businesses with a powerful and authentic noble purpose.

The business sells ...	**Which means to the potential customer ...**
Safety (e.g., Mercedes Benz)	Security
Brainpower (e.g., Data3)	Efficiency
Time savings (e.g., Domino's Pizza)	Convenience
Hope (e.g., Cochlear)	Relief (i.e., solving a problem)

Other key business components to investigate

Having obtained a high-level view, we can now delve into each business by asking:

- What does it produce or offer in the way of services?
- What are its best-selling products or services and why?
- How is it different, or better, than its peers?
- What competition exists and how does it differentiate itself?

- Are there any international competitors who could potentially open operations in Australia? For example, the Amazon effect on local retailers?

It is not always the obvious product or service that is marketed by a business. Many people think of McDonald's® as a restaurant that makes money solely from selling hamburgers. However, all of their outlets around the world owned by McDonald's®, and leased to franchisees, account for over 20% of their revenue. As such, they could equally be considered a real estate business.

I think deeply about how a business *really* makes its money. What *needs* does the business serve? To get to the core of what a business does, think of the emotional impact that need fulfills. Using McDonald's® again, as an example, its product serves a need to provide a meal easily, quickly, and cheaply.

Other Qualitative Factors to Consider

Competition

Investors are sometimes discouraged by the effects of competition on the businesses they own. However, competition is healthy, encouraging innovation and greater effort as opposed to monopolies with market domination and no incentive to improve.

Management

When an event like the GFC occurs, poorly managed businesses are more prone to failure or being procured by a rival.

Understanding

The simpler the business model, the easier it will be to grasp, such as Woolworths. Only invest in more complex businesses, such as those in IT, if you have a clear understanding of their business operations and associated risks.

Contracts

Businesses surviving on contracts are termed 'book and burn', which means they are only as good as their next contract. If they are winning a considerable number of contracts, could they be undercutting their competitors too aggressively to win the business?

When the media, or the business itself, announces with great fanfare the winning of a significant contract, it raises a red flag for me. It's pointless winning a $100 million contract if it may cost $120 million to implement. Before committing to an investment that relies on income from contracts, look at the magnitude and success rate of their previous contracts.

The once-successful WA mining services business Forge® is an example. With the advent of two major contract over-runs, and other managerial issues, Forge fell into liquidation in early 2014.[45]

Acquisitions

CEOs are often under pressure to expand the business and could fall victim to venture capitalists with offers of merger bargains. The CEO's decision might also be ego-driven as, with a merger, they could potentially progress from managing a medium-sized business (by market capitalisation) to a much larger one. This is covered in depth in the chapter 'The Effect of CEOs and Board Members on Wealth Winners®' from the book *Finding Wealth Winners® the Teaminvest Way*.[46]

As we now know, a business can grow organically and/or by making acquisitions. However, recognise that acquisitions can be risky: Hewlett Packard® purchased Palm Pilot for over $1b in April 2010 and it appears to have underestimated the impact of the iPhone®—launched a few years earlier—with the result that the Palm Pilot technology soon became redundant.

Detailed research of the business

Experience their products or services

It's helpful to become familiar with the businesses and their associated products and services. If there are stores, visit their outlets, experience their service firsthand, and observe their culture. Where possible, engage with members of staff and ask casual questions around the management and business. Enquire whether they've invested in the business themselves.

Ask anyone who may be a customer why they favour this business over a competitor.

And remember to assess the business through an investor's eyes, not merely as a consumer.

Avoid the media noise

Media-driven share market updates are based primarily on daily share price movements and are intended to cause excitement or invoke fear. Long-term value investors, on the other hand, can ignore all the busyness of everyday reporting while they wait for the business results which become available every six months in Australia (or every quarter in the US).

Announcements

In addition to the company reports, it is possible, and important, to digest the business announcements of our prospective investments via the ASX or Listcorp®. By focusing on price-sensitive announcements, of particular interest to investors, we can avoid information overload.

Third party transactions

Pay attention to any third-party related transactions, as detailed in the annual report and notes. They could include items such as a board member steering work to other businesses they are connected with—which could legitimately be construed as a conflict of interest.

Investing outside Australia

The US share market has outpaced the ASX for the last ten years, so Australian investors may feel the desire to diversify abroad. While it is possible to purchase shares in foreign businesses, we are unlikely to be as familiar with their operations and this creates a certain element of risk. Perhaps consider purchasing shares in an Australian business that derives a portion of its income from abroad. Some ASX-listed businesses that derive more than 50% of their income overseas are Cochlear, CSL, ResMed, and Domino's.

Chapter Summary

We have spent some time exploring what makes a business tick. Factually, we can read the annual and interim reports and business announcements, being wary of media noise. Practically, we can get a feel for the business and its culture by visiting outlets or trying their products or services. It's highly beneficial to get as close to the business and its people as possible.

Activity: From your list of prospective businesses, work through a 'SWOT' analysis to identify key *strengths, weaknesses, opportunities,* and *threats* to each business. It may help to think of strengths and weaknesses as the internal factors and opportunities and threats as the external factors.

Does each business present a clear and concise statement about its brand, purpose, or vision which is more than simply describing its products/services? Does it appear to derive its strategy and direction from this statement?

Notes

....

....

....

....

....

....

....

....

....

....

....

....

Chapter 6
Company Management

It is vital we believe in the trustworthiness of the board and management before, and after, we invest in any business. As Warren Buffett succinctly comments: 'You can't make a good deal with a bad person.'[47]

Factors to Determine Whether Management is Trustworthy

Past record

Do they have an acceptable professional record in any previous roles? Assess the longevity of the board members and how they and the CEO managed past economic cycles, including any crises.

Capital raising

If they undertook a capital raising, try to ascertain the reason. How is this additional capital to be used? Could it disadvantage shareholders in addition to the dilution effect on earnings per share?

Acquisitions

Based on historical annual reports, were there any acquisitions? Were they in line with the business model, and did earnings increase as a result?

Share buybacks

How did they pay for a share buyback—with excess cash, or did they incur debt? Did the reason supplied for the buyback seem rational to you?

Overseas expansion

Did they undertake any unsuccessful or failed overseas expansions?

Integrity

Has there been a long tenure by the business board and management? Do they appear to have a high level of integrity in your opinion?

Skin in the game

Did any executive members purchase shares in the business, outside of their incentives? Are any of them major shareholders in the business?

Teaminvest members applaud management with 'skin in the game'. This term relates to the number of shares personally purchased by executives and it demonstrates their level of faith in the business. As it is difficult to establish whether shareholdings are purchased or received as part of an incentive, I am more interested in whether the shareholdings are retained or whether they are being disposed of regularly and/or recently.

General complacency

Are they failing to recognise or adapt to changing competitive landscapes, similar to Kodak failing to recognise the power of digital photography?

Poor decisions

Has the management made any unsuccessful strategic moves, such as the Woolworths failed expansion into hardware with Masters?

Outcome

Has there been any significant changes to the key financial metrics? What explanations were provided?

A book called *The Founders Mentality* by Zook and Allen (2016) expands on the subject of why businesses with their original founder still in charge are often better managed and more motivated. By contrast, hired professional management may be reticent to purchase shares themselves and instead rely on receiving shares as a bonus, or via options as part of their incentive packages. Some successful businesses still retain their original founders at the helm or continue to be led by management with a strong founder mentality:

- Flight Centre—Graham Turner
- Technology One—Adrian di Marco
- ARB—The Brown brothers
- Apple, the first US trillion-dollar business—built by Steve Jobs and now managed by long-time employee, Tim Cooke
- Amazon—Jeff Bezos
- Berkshire Hathaway—Warren Buffett and Charlie Munger.

Tip

Berkshire Hathaway is one of the most successful and enduring businesses in the world and yet, surprisingly, its share price has dropped by more than 50% on four occasions. These

> drops occurred in 1974, 1987, 1998, and 2009. The most recent was during the GFC when the overall market fell over 51%, inevitably dragging down most businesses. Despite the falls, Berkshire's share price has grown from $7.50 in December 1962 to $472,257 as of February 2022. It is a clear reminder to maintain faith in our research and patience with our investments. Provided earnings continue to grow, a business's share price should eventually follow.

Annual General Meetings

By investing in a business, we become part owners and the management and board report to us at their annual general meeting. The interim report and announcements fill the information gaps between meetings. The management are custodians of our business, and we have a right to know how diligent they are in the stewardship of our funds.

Once I become a part-owner of a business, I look forward to attending every AGM and benefitting from a wonderful insight into the people on the management team and the board.

Prior to the AGM, it is helpful to assess the congruency of the chairman and CEO's previous reports with the most recent. With research, we can assess individual performance levels and thereby increase our knowledge and familiarity with management.

It is also worthwhile studying the remuneration section within the annual report to determine which metrics and incentives are applied for senior management's remuneration packages. The report can be assessed in terms of clarity, alignment, and quantum, which are elaborated on in the coming chapters.

The difficulty in accurately assessing the quality of management can be somewhat mitigated by attending AGMs. While at a meeting, pay close attention to what is said and how messages are delivered. Pay attention to described plans for future growth and intended strategies to achieve them. Observe whether the key personnel present themselves in an open, honest, and rational manner. Shareholders expect the CEO and board to focus on how they will grow profits going forward. Take note if this is excluded.

Does management speak highly of their staff and the contributions they bring to the business? Are they honest about their mistakes and acknowledge where their weaknesses lie? Does management blame external circumstances for their failings or tend to seek regulatory protection or financial assistance from the government?

Aside from the numbers presented by the chairman and CEO, the nuances of tone and body language can be more revealing to attentive observers.

Observe whether the management encourages shareholder questions or are they reluctant to accommodate them? Are they open and willing or arrogant and evasive?

Interactions with the CEO and board should boost confidence in their ability to run a successful business. After every AGM, I take the time to stay for a cuppa and raise some questions:

- Board member—why did you choose to be on the board for XYZ business?
- CEO—what keeps you awake at night?
- Staff member—what do you like most about working for business XYZ?

- Fellow investor—what headwinds do you foresee in XYZ business?
- Supplier/customer—what is the business like to deal with?

I recall attending an AGM where the management invited us for tea and a chat after the event, as is common practice. However, they avoided mingling with their investors and slipped out soon after the presentation. My fellow Teaminvest investors and I were distinctly dismayed by this arrogance and, having lost faith in the management, I sold my shares in the business. This lack of congruency can be a more valid reason to sell a holding than a drop in share price.

As shareholders, we expand our knowledge of a business by attending an AGM, and it is a terrific opportunity to determine whether the board and management are, indeed, good stewards of our capital.

Most Australian businesses hold their AGMs in the months following the end of financial year on 30 June. Interim results are announced as at the end of the calendar year. A few others, including several banks, report their interim at the end of March and annual at the end of September.

Chapter Summary

The integrity and quality of the management team in charge of running a business have a significant long-term impact on its performance. For a better understanding of the people with this responsibility, it's highly recommended to become a serial AGM attender. Take the opportunity to engage with members of the management and board and use your senses and intuition to gauge whether you are indeed comfortable and confident that there is no reason to distrust management.

Activity: Look at the businesses in your shortlist/ portfolio—after further research on the board and management, do you remain comfortable with their stewardship of your investment?

Notes

....

....

....

....

....

....

....

....

....

....

....

....

....

....

....

....

Chapter 7
Remuneration Report

The remuneration (Rem) report is contained within the annual report and is a powerful tool for understanding the goals and objectives the board has set for the CEO and management to achieve. I am grateful to Howard Coleman (director and co-founder of Teaminvest), for impressing upon me the importance of the Rem report and its ramifications on the board and management in any business.

Imagine if a friend asked you to invest in their business and provided everything you needed to know about the business yet declined to divulge how they intended to remunerate themselves. Would you be comfortable with this?

Yet, somehow, we as investors place our cash and trust in publicly listed businesses every day without seeking an answer to this important question. Why? In many cases, it feels just too daunting. So let me help by guiding you through this revealing report.

Understanding the Remuneration Report

Most remuneration reports are either too long and complex for easy understanding or merely boilerplate; that is, they follow a standardised template usually set up by external consultants. A shining example of a clear and succinct remuneration report is that produced by ARB, at just two pages long. By comparison, some listed businesses of a comparable size produce reports that exceed thirty pages in length. The longer and more convoluted the report, the more sceptical I become. When reading a Rem report, we look at three specific aspects:

1. Clarity: is it clear and understandable?
2. Quantum: is remuneration reasonable given the size and complexity of the business?
3. Alignment: does it motivate management to achieve what shareholders desire?

This is where the rubber hits the road—professional or hired boards and management can sometimes differ from founder-driven businesses in their focus on personal benefits over the growth of the business. Business founders tend to be more circumspect when it comes to self-reward and maintain a strong emotional tie and considerable pride in the ongoing success of the business they built.

When looking at the Rem report, think about it from a clarity, quantum, and alignment point of view:

Clarity

The Rem report should be clear, transparent, understandable, and easy to read. We do not like the Rem report to be overly complicated, for example using Monte Carlo or binomial measures, which are formula-based and difficult to understand.

Quantum

The amount paid to management should equate to the size and complexity of the business, and a comparison to its peers helps in this regard.

Alignment

The hurdles or benchmarks should align the management with growing the business and should incentivise them to do this. It's especially important to understand how the management and board are paid because it reflects their level of devotion to the success of the business. Are the hurdles or benchmarks too easily achieved? We prefer to see them set as an incentive towards driving results.

We also believe it's more beneficial for management to receive a bonus based on improving a business's earnings over the long term rather than increasing the business's share price. The Rem report should outline the conditions of the short-term incentives as well as long-term incentives, and we prefer the management not to be overly tempted by the short-term incentives at the expense of long-term results.

As much as the Australian Hayne Royal Commission revealed the poor and unsavoury practices of some in the financial sector, investors have always had the opportunity to raise questions or object to anomalies in the remuneration report at AGMs. While we can legitimately expect a level of integrity and professionalism in a business's reports, we should also be willing to undertake our own checks and balances.

Compare Remuneration Reports

Compare a business's Rem report for the past few years to verify how consistent it has been. If there has been a change of CEO, compare the new remuneration package with that of the previous CEO and be alert to any significant increases.

The Rem report should be aligned to business strategy. For example, if the CEO states in their report they aim to achieve a specific growth of earnings, then the respective benchmark or hurdle to receive a bonus should be based on the EPS itself, rather than on soft or vague hurdles.

Although the growth of earnings is a laudable criterion to incentivise management, this growth may be achieved by acquiring new businesses, and it is only possible to ascertain what real value has been added to the business in the years following the acquisition.

The introduction of the 2011 'two strikes and you're out' policy has made businesses more aware of excessive salaries and bonuses. It has forced them to be clearer in stipulating management income and the required benchmarks. While remuneration reports have become more standardised due to the proliferation of remuneration consultants in the marketplace, investors should still become familiar with the format and study them carefully.

Components of the Remuneration Report

Terms frequently referred to in the Rem report include key management personnel (KMP)—the people who are key to the business—and key performance indicators (KPI)—the hurdles or benchmarks that must be achieved for management to reach their targets. Sadly, these hurdles are often not clear, or expanded upon, so seek clarification at an AGM and take note of how openly the CEO responds.

Normally, the remuneration report is split into three parts:

- Fixed salary or fixed annual remuneration (FAR).
- Short-term incentives (STI) normally set as targets the preceding year and generally paid out in cash.
- Long-term incentives (LTI) normally set three years in advance. Often LTIs include an option of shares in the business. Look for a clawback policy, which allows a board to withdraw shares granted as

options for reasons such as fraud or dishonesty. Imagine how effective a clawback clause might have been during the GFC, where many managers walked away with their bonuses intact, despite the collapse of the businesses they managed.

The remuneration split is normally FAR 45%, STI 15%, and LTI 40%. The higher the LTI, the better for long-term investors, as it incentivises management to a longer-term commitment. So-called *professional boards* are often more susceptible to self-interest and being able to claim their incentives in a relatively brief period.

Consider the value of the total incentives compared to the total earnings of the business. If it appears disproportionate, compare the factor with its peers.

Tip

Long-term incentives (LTIs) often include options in the business. The prices quoted in the report may be benchmarked against Monte Carlo or binomial measures which are formula-based and difficult to understand. As we seek clarity and transparency in remuneration reports, we would generally avoid a business that uses these measures.

To ensure the commitment of management, the KPIs should be linked to, and measured against, business outcomes. Take notice of any vagueness in how KPIs are set.

Make-up of the Board

The smaller the board the better, as bloated boards are costly to a business and can dilute the responsibility and accountability of the members. We prefer a board size of between 5 and 7 members.

There appears to be an increasing preference for short-term tenure on the board, as recommended by some proxy advisors and industry associations. We prefer business directors to remain on the board for many years provided they are delivering on their promises. The better board members spend years cultivating their knowledge of the business and improving their professional networks. There can surely be no benefit in introducing new blood simply for the sake of it, if a board has already proven its competence.

When flying commercially overseas, many passengers would take comfort from a mature airline captain with grey hair, suggesting many years of flying experience.

Another trend of concern is the appointment of independent non-executive directors. Let's take a simple hypothetical example: Richmond football club won the AFL Premiership in 2019 and 2020. If the current Richmond FC board was replaced by independent directors, it may end up consisting of members with a knowledge of other sports but an insufficient collective knowledge of footy. As such, it would become hard to envisage the club winning another premiership.

Proxy agencies can influence votes quite substantially by touting for the voting support of investors and institutions. Although it might provide a convenient solution for many, it isn't necessarily in the best interest of the business. Investors need to commit the time and effort to make their own decisions on such important matters rather than absolve their individual responsibility to proxy agencies.

Chapter Summary

It's a worthwhile endeavour to become familiar with the format and contents of the remuneration report within a company's annual report. This document can reveal valuable information about the business culture and how it evaluates and rewards its management.

Activity: Look at the businesses in your portfolio, noting the complexity and length of their remuneration reports, and satisfy yourself that they are clear, fair, and align with the business objectives.

Notes

....

....

....

....

....

....

....

....

....

....

....

....

....

....

Chapter 8
Moats

The word moat originates from the days of medieval castles which were protected from invaders by deep trenches filled with water. The wider and deeper the moat, the safer the ruler felt. In business, this metaphor applies where a business replaces the castle, and the moats are able to protect the business from its competitors. Coca-Cola® has a strong moat in its closely guarded secret formula, which provides the business with a sustainable competitive advantage over its peers and acts as a barrier to entry to new players in the soft drink market.

Teaminvest considers a moat to be a readily identified attribute of a business, preferably unique, that increases confidence in its earnings per share growing at least as fast as inflation over the next economic cycle (5–7 years).

As Buffett describes it:

> *Our long-term competitive position improves as a result of these almost unnoticeable actions [...] essential if we are to have the kind of business we want a decade or two from now. We always, of course, hope to earn more money in the short-term. But when short-term and long-term conflict, widening the moat must take precedence.*[48]

A particularly strong moat is the trapdoor moat which is sometimes also described as being 'sticky'. Health insurance companies and banks are sometimes said to benefit from a trapdoor moat because it is such a hassle to change providers that customers simply stay put, despite there being better deals available.

Other moats include 'first mover advantage' businesses that are the quickest to react to changing trends and technology. Innovative and forward-thinking companies which established themselves early in their marketplace include REA Group®, Carsales®, and Facebook®.

A well-established business with good moats could expect a strong earnings growth, certainly well above inflation. Moats are ideally deep and durable, such as patents, which take an enormous effort and cost to attain and can last many years.

An insight into the moats regarded by the board and management as protecting their business can be gleaned from the annual reports and any recent presentations.

Buffett explains other attributes keeping competitors at bay: 'A formidable barrier such as a business being a low-cost producer (GEICO, Costco®) or possessing a powerful world-wide brand (Coca-Cola, Gillette®, American Express) is essential for sustained success.'[49]

Types of Moats

Structural

Moat	Business example
Being the lowest-cost provider	JB Hi-Fi®, The Reject Shop®
Long-term contracts in place	Monadelphous®
Holding patents or licences	CSL, Cochlear, ResMed

Geographic

A spread of retail outlets in key locations throughout the country and the world: Westfield®, Accent Group, Nick Scali®.

Location

A prime site with supporting infrastructure and accessibility: Woolworths and Coles®.

Trapdoor

Difficult to change from one vendor to another: Technology One, NIB Holdings Ltd, and commercial banks.

Network effect

Robust networks: Realestate.com, Carsales®, Facebook®. Telstra® lost its network effect when fixed phone lines were largely replaced by mobile phones.

Reputational or brand

Moat	Business example
Brand names with high recognition	Google®
Reputable products/services.	Apple, ARB, Cochlear

Founder mentality or strategy

Moat	Business example
High value continually being added due to the direct influence of the founder	Adrian di Marco of Technology One; Rene Sugo of Symbio; Jamie Pherous of Corporate Travel Management Group

Managerial

The CEO has a proven track record of adding extraordinary shareholder value such as the Brown brothers at ARB and the dynamic entrepreneur Chris Ellison at Mineral Resources Ltd.

Processes

Where an easily replicated business model leads a business to successful franchises such as McDonald's and Domino's Pizza.

Patent or technology

These moats provide strong barriers to entry that are difficult to breach and remain durable for many years. Cochlear does this well with its superior technology, patents, and approvals for products granted by health regulators, not easily emulated by potential competitors.

Low-cost provider

A business that can produce a product or provide a service that has a very low cost or price. The popularity of Domino's Pizzas makes it difficult for others to enter into the fast-food market.

Closely Monitor Moats

All business moats need to be thoroughly reviewed whenever there are company announcements and when looking at interim and annual results. If any of the moats are weakened, or have been breached, this could reduce our confidence that the EPS will continue to grow at least as fast as inflation.

In 2011, Cochlear had a potentially serious product recall. One could expect its product moat had been breached. However, the company held an extraordinary general meeting (EGM) and showed that it was able to manage the crisis with minimal damage to its business.

Chapter Summary

Successful businesses strive for a competitive and sustainable advantage over their peers to maintain their position and relevance. These advantages can become durable and impenetrable moats in a business sense. Moats need to be monitored over time to ensure they have not weakened or been breached.

Activity: Identify three moats for each business in your portfolio and keep a log of them. Every six months when the business reports, try to determine if they have been strengthened or weakened. Measure each by their depth and durability.

Notes

....

....

....

....

....

....

....

Chapter 9
Risks

In the same way as we analyse moats, we consider the risks associated with investing in a business. They are categorised below:

Business risks may be influenced by the quality and competence of the management, such as changes in CEO or loss of reputation. A brand could suffer from a lawsuit; a sector such as resources could fall out of favour due to climate change concerns; technology could become outdated; competitors may irrationally drop prices; moats could become eroded.

Market risks relate to challenges within the industry and sector the business operates in. These could include changes in inflation and interest rates, conflicts, and regulatory amendments.

External risks are threats, such as the COVID pandemic, which are beyond the control of the business. Others to consider would be sovereign, economic, regulatory, environmental, social, or disruptive competition.

We need to identify as many risks as possible which could have the potential to weaken the continuing success of a business's operations. Each moat that has been identified will have associated risks.

We collectively assess the likelihood of each risk occurring over the next economic cycle (5–7 years) and the potential damage to the business should the risk occur.

In the USA, the annual reports highlight business risks, a practice that is now becoming more common in Australia.

Technological Disruption

In such a modern and ever-changing world, technology risks are some of the greatest disrupters to consider:

- How could technology replace a product/service a business is providing?
- Are the businesses themselves embracing technology and can they switch over easily?

Many businesses are affected by technological disruption. A profound example is Kodak, who invented the digital camera but failed to take advantage of the rising popularity of digital photography. When the smartphone introduced its inbuilt capability to take, view, and share digital images, it negated the need for printed copies. The popular tagline 'A Kodak moment' is often quoted when businesses fail to pivot or recognise technological changes. Woolworths proactively embraced technology by introducing online ordering and home delivery of supermarket items.

Components of Risk

Having identified and determined the likelihood of the risks occurring and the potential damage to the business, the ensuing discussion helps us to evaluate the significance of these risks. For example, if we were considering investing in Woolworths, the likelihood of shoplifting is quite high, yet the damage to the business is likely to be low, so we may not feel unduly concerned.

By contrast, consider the oil and gas company BP and the likelihood of another major oil spill. I would argue that, assuming safety measures were implemented following the last disaster, the probability of the risk occurring again would be quite low. However, if the risk did indeed materialise, the damage would be immense, quite conceivably making us less willing to invest in the business.

The free climber, Alex Honnold, was the first person to ascend El Capitan in Yosemite National Park without aids of any kind. His story is magnificently portrayed in the film *Free Solo*. Alex has the following to say about risk:

> *I considered every possibility while I was on the ground. There was no room for doubt to creep in. Doubt is a precursor to fear. Visualise, rehearse and remove all doubts.*[50]

And

> *If I get an adrenaline rush there is something incredibly wrong.*[51]

Learning from Alex's philosophy, consider the worst-case scenario of predetermined risks materialising *before* committing to your investment, and decide, in advance, the action you *will* take should any occur. As part of my own emotional preparation prior to a share purchase, I consider each business risk as if it has just occurred and decide the best action to take:

- Sell my shares immediately
- Hold on
- Buy more, should the price drop.

Another example of risk assessment is that many people drive SUVs because of their more robust build and enhanced feeling of safety. This might tempt them, however, to drive more recklessly and could contribute to a higher fatality rate in SUVs.

Being impervious to risk could also tempt an investor into entering a strongly rising market, called a bull market. Buffett cautions: 'Risk comes from not knowing what you're doing'.[52]

Human Biases

At the beginning of the book, I discussed mindset and biases. Our biases could provide an insight on how we might manage, and cope with, the risks of investing in a fluctuating share market. Are we emotionally and practically prepared if our portfolio were to drop in share price by 50%? Right now, try to imagine this scenario and how it would feel. You may even experience some physical fear or panic at the mere prospect of a significant financial loss.

To ride out storms, my own strategy is to ensure the cash committed in my investments will not be urgently required in the short term. I aim to set aside two years' worth of living expenses to avoid any undue pressure to sell an investment prematurely.

There can be an overlap between the biases covered earlier in the book and how we perceive and manage risk:

1. **Put things into perspective.**
   We may sometimes feel that the world is in such a state of flux that it's too risky to commit to any new venture or, for that matter, invest our capital into a share market that has been significantly affected by the COVID pandemic. Try to visualise how hopeless the future may have felt for those living with the stresses and insecurities of the Second World War, which lasted a gruelling six years. Our current challenges could be considered insignificant by comparison.

Remember the biases from Chapter 1? This is an example of 'recency bias'.

2. **Think about the articles we are reading and their source.**
   We receive information constantly and instantly from so many sources nowadays it is quite easy to become overwhelmed. Stick to reliable and reputable media sources, and you may notice that less is better. Be particularly discerning when you find yourself aligning with information that supports your own point of view as this can become confirmation bias. Remain open to contrarian information and opinions.
3. **It's still a big world.**
   Having become more connected than ever before, and with quicker and easier access to information, we could find it increasingly difficult to maintain a focus on what is relevant to our investing goals. Consciously resist being drawn in and distracted by daily share price fluctuations and other superfluous noise. Not all information is equal, nor is more information necessarily better than less.
4. **Volatility.**
   We understand the share market can be volatile, especially in the short term, and we could become fearful in anticipation of capital losses. Loss aversion can lead to missing opportunities and become detrimental to our investing outcomes. Have a predetermined plan and take appropriate action. Dithering, and making no decision, is still a decision.
5. **Distractions.**
   The daily share price fluctuations, volatility, bull and bear markets, and predictions of crashes are

the primary focus of most reports and news items. While these could be distracting, long-term value investors remain slow and steady, maintaining their focus on the business earnings and fundamentals.

Sometimes a sudden price drop can be caused by shorters, who benefit from falling share prices. Shorters often trade for the short-term, and they specialise in exposing price-sensitive weaknesses within a business. The fallout can inadvertently provide an opportunity for long-term investors who understand the business and are ready to capitalise on investing in a great business at a lower price.

Chapter Summary

No investment in the share market is entirely without risk. Before acting on an investment opportunity, we should consider all types of risks that could befall the business. Once risks have been identified, we should know in advance how we will react should any of them be triggered. Forewarned is forearmed in this instance.

Activity: Identify three risks for each of the investments you currently hold and, against each one, record an unemotional action we intend to take, should the risk eventuate.

Notes

Chapter 10
Step 3—Purchase Price

My goal as a value investor is to purchase a holding in businesses at a sensible price, with confidence the future growth of earnings will provide me with my desired return. The return should exceed inflation, at the minimum, and mitigate the risk of transferring capital from the bank to the share market. To substantiate this, the average market return over the past seventy years has been 11.7% pa and 9.2% pa over the last thirty years.[17]

Share market volatility is driven by sentiment and is influenced by conflicts, pending elections, a change in interest rates, or a downturn in economic conditions, natural disasters, and, most recently, a pandemic.

Be aware that the smaller portfolios held by concentrated investors will be more volatile than the All-Ordinaries Index. This would be like a small speedboat and a large ship battling the same choppy sea. Volatility could easily amplify emotions (and seasickness!) associated with loss aversion, and a solid long-term view of a business will help to mitigate this. Shift your focus to a longer time frame and take direction from announcements and financial reports.

The two methods of assessing businesses for potential investments are:

1. Fundamental: the study of business financials.
2. Technical: the analysis of share price movements on charts.

Teaminvest focuses solely on fundamental analysis. Personally, I consult a price chart albeit briefly, over the longest possible period, to gain an indication of the overall trend of a business and how it has been driven by market sentiment.

Baron Rothschild, an 18th-century British nobleman and member of the Rothschild banking family, coined the quote 'the time to buy is when there's blood in the streets.'[53]

Understandably, this is easier said than done and is the main reason I devoted an entire chapter to mindset and temperament.

It's advisable to maintain an overall awareness of prevailing interest rates and economic conditions to assist in understanding the market as a whole. As a rule, PEs are driven up when bank interest rates are low as investors turn to share market investments for better returns. Always remember we are investing in a business—NOT the market.

Capital gain is derived from the growth of earnings, so we aim for gains to exceed 3%. This is considered the maximum inflation Reserve Bank is comfortable with.

> Earnings yield = (Earnings ÷ Share Price) x 100
> (Inverse of PE)

> Dividend yield = (Annual Dividend per share ÷ Price per share) x 100

As an example, business XYZ has a PE of 15, so its earnings yield (1 ÷ 15) is 6.7%. Therefore, if its dividend yield is 4%, the potential total shareholder return (dividend plus capital gain) is 6.7% (2.7% + 4%). The 10-year average dividend yield for the ASX 300 is 4.6% per annum.[16] It is important to recognise how the compounding effect can impact your wealth over time. The graph on the next page illustrates this well.

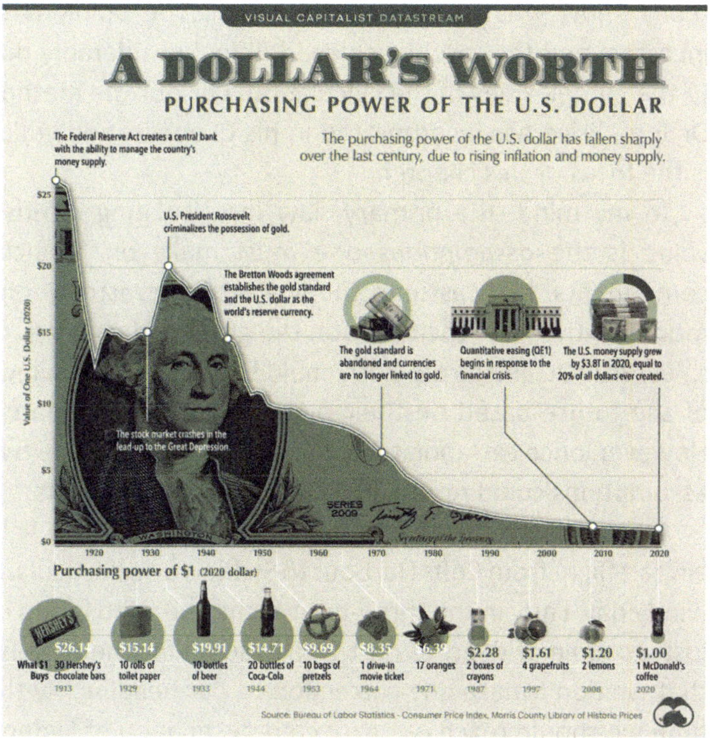

Figure 26—Purchasing power of the US Dollar (1931–2021) [54]

Compounding can work in both directions. Since the US Federal Reserve was created in 1913 and given control over the nation's money supply, the Consumer Price Index has increased by a factor of 27.25 times. This has caused the US Dollar to lose 96.3% of its value/purchasing power.

Okay, so we know what return we can expect, and the impact of compounding, so let's find out the price to pay that will help us achieve what we want from our investment. In determining a sensible purchase price, we need to know a business's current worth—its intrinsic value. There are potentially several methods to determine the intrinsic value of a business. I say potentially as how can anyone *really* know what a business is worth. The opinions of investors and the results achieved differ considerably due to the complexities of the calculation. I favour the method Dr John Price has incorporated in his CI application which is the focus of this chapter.

To my mind, the primary flaw in calculating intrinsic value is the *assumptions* one must make on financial components. Let's assume there are two investors—one more positive than the other on the growth of earnings or sales/PE/ROE and so on. Both could fully justify their views of the future based on their own independent research. However, once extrapolated, any small disparity in the two assumptions could return significantly different results.

An analogy that comes to mind is embarking on a light aircraft flight from Coffs Harbour to Sydney, on a particularly windy day. Early in the three-hour flight, the wind blows us just a couple of degrees off track. Assume for the exercise that we don't make any correction to our heading. By the time we should reach our expected destination of Sydney, we could find ourselves significantly off track, perhaps over the Blue Mountains!

The subjective nature of value calculations might also explain why analysts from various broking houses can present contrasting estimates albeit with a small difference in their assumptions.

With this in mind, how can we expect to ever reach an accurate intrinsic value figure? We may be better to take the past results of the business into account and project forwards from that as a guide. It is a logical way of viewing the future and aligns with the methodology proposed by Dr John Price and incorporated in his CI application. What follows has been my own personal investing epiphany!

Margin of Safety

To my mind, this is a vital component in achieving exemplary returns. The following Buffett quote may help to elucidate the principle of the margin of safety:

> You don't try to buy businesses worth $83 million for $80 million. You leave yourself an enormous margin [of safety]. When you build a bridge, you insist it can carry 30,000 pounds, but you only drive 10,000-pound trucks across it. And that same principle works in investing.[55]

Our own local experience of this is the audacious construction of the Sydney Harbour Bridge in 1932, then the tallest and widest steel arch bridge in the world. Before opening the bridge to normal traffic, the engineers tested its strength with an impressive margin of safety—fifty steam locomotives parked along the length of the bridge at the same time.

An automated margin of safety calculation has been incorporated into the CI application and is an invaluable tool for investors when preparing to purchase parcels of shares.

Using the return screen from CI, the following sequence of snapshots will reveal how a sensible buy price, with a margin of safety, can be achieved.

	Based on Past 5 Years	
	DEFAULT	SAFETY
Price $	9.47	9.47
EPSttm $	0.22	0.22
P/E Ratio	38.69	30.99
HGrowth %	11.92	5.8
Payout %	67.5	65.7
STRETD® %	11.87	1.54
Req. return %	10	10
TARGD® $	10.30	6.35

*Note: algorithms are involved

Figure 27—The average performance of Technology One over the past five years

An explanation of the key financial ratios in the return calculations.

	DEFAULT	SAFETY	
Price $	9.47	9.47	Closing Price
EPSttm $	0.22	0.22	Earnings per share Trailing Twelve Months
P/E Ratio	38.69	30.99	Price to Earnings
HGrowth %	11.92	5.8	Historical Growth of Earnings
Payout %	67.5	65.7	Payout ratio
STRETD® %	11.87	1.54	
Req. return %	10	10	
TARGD® $	10.30	6.35	

Figure 28—The key metrics used in the return calculations

The growth of earnings is a measure of the business, the payout ratio is a measure of the management and board, and the PE is a measure of market sentiment.

	DEFAULT	
Price $	9.47	If purchased at **$9.47** ...
EPSttm $	0.22	
P/E Ratio	38.69	and if historical performance continues ...
HGrowth %	11.92	
Payout %	67.5	
STRETD® %	11.87	anticipate a return of **11.87%** pa
Req. return %	10	
TARGD® $	10.30	

STRETD®—Stock Return with Dividends reinvested.

Figure 29—An example of how to determine the expected return from the current share price

	DEFAULT	
Price $	9.47	
EPSttm $	0.22	
P/E Ratio	38.69	
HGrowth %	11.92	
Payout %	67.5	
STRETD® %	11.87	
Req. return %	**10**	For a Required Return of **10%** pa pay ...
TARGD® $	**10.30**	no more than **$10.30** Target Price

TARGD® = Target price with dividends reinvested

Figure 30—A target price is provided for a default 10% return

The application defaults the required rate of return to 10%. This can be manually changed to the desired return for each business, based on the significance of the identified risks or moats.

Now let's add a margin of safety. Algorithms automatically stress-test the three key financial ratios by incorporating any negative anomalies found over the past five years.

	DEFAULT	SAFETY
Price $		9.47
EPSttm $		0.22
P/E Ratio	38.69	30.99
HGrowth %		5.8
Payout %		65.7
STRETD® %		1.54
Req. return %		10
TARGD® $		6.35

P / E: 5-year average **38.69**, 'stress' tested = **30.99**

Figure 31—A worst case or stressed P/E is calculated

	DEFAULT	SAFETY
Price $		9.47
EPSttm $		0.22
P/E Ratio		30.99
HGrowth %	11.92	5.8
Payout %		65.7
STRETD® %		1.54
Req. return %		10
TARGD® $		6.35

Growth of Earnings: **11.92%**, 'stress' tested = **5.8%**

Figure 32—A worst case or stressed growth of earnings is calculated

	DEFAULT	SAFETY
Price $		9.47
EPSttm $		0.22
P/E Ratio		30.99
HGrowth %		5.8
Payout %	67.5	65.7
STRETD® %		1.54
Req. return %		10
TARGD® $		6.35

Payout: **67.5%**, 'stress' tested = **65.7%**

Figure 33—A more conservative or stressed payout ratio is calculated

	DEFAULT	SAFETY	
Price $		9.47	If purchased at **$9.47** …
EPSttm $		0.22	
			and if historical performance
P/E Ratio		30.99	continues …
HGrowth %		5.8	
Payout %		65.7	
			anticipate a 'stress' tested return
STRETD® %		1.54	of **1.54%** pa
Req. return %		10	
TARGD® $		6.35	

Figure 34—A stock return figure called STRETD® is calculated

	DEFAULT	SAFETY	
Price $		9.47	
EPSttm $		0.22	
P/E Ratio		30.99	
HGrowth %		5.8	
Payout %		65.7	
STRETD® %		1.54	
Req. return %		10	For a Required Return of **10%** pa pay ...
TARGD® $		6.35	no more than **$6.35** Target Price

Figure 35—A target price called TARGD® is calculated for a 10% return

In conclusion, we should attempt to purchase shares at the target (TARGD®) buy price, with an additional margin of safety, being $6.35. Based on your own research, you may wish to adjust any of the ratios, and your required rate of return, to suit a differing viewpoint.

An investor should only consider purchasing shares at a higher price than the margin of safety if they have good reason to believe the growth of earnings will increase at a faster rate in the future. This will, however, make the purchase more susceptible to any short-term correction or pull back.

The PE as a Check and Balance

It is possible within the application to compare the current PE to the average PE over the past four years to determine its current position within this range. If the current PE falls to within the bottom third of the average range, it is considered a sensible price to pay.

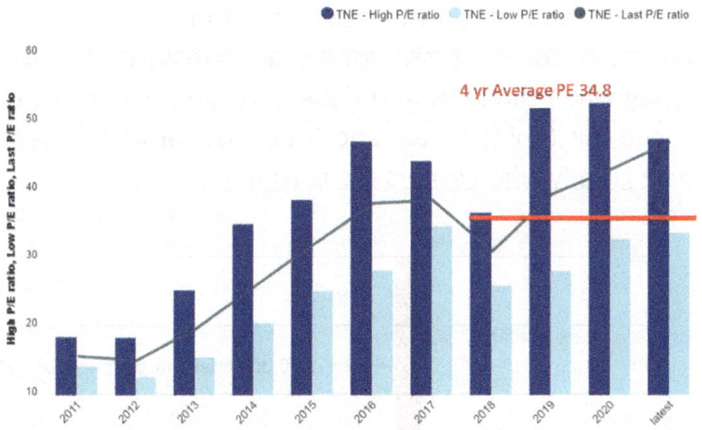

Figure 36—High/low PE and Last (average) PE[56]

While this chart shows the high and low PE for the past ten years, Dr John Price's research indicates that a four-year period is more than adequate for this measure. The average PE over four years is condensed into a simple format below.

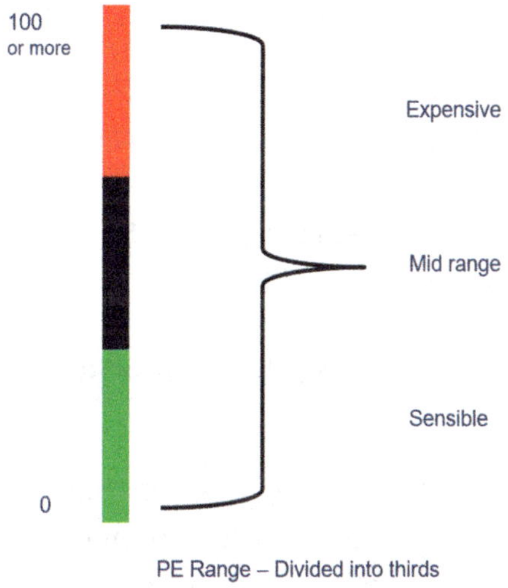

Figure 37—PE range

If a PE is too high (in the black or red range), it could be considered too expensive for a share purchase. We prefer to buy when the PE is in the green range. Teaminvest has named this tool the 'Fear and Greed Indicator'. It is better to be greedy when others are fearful.

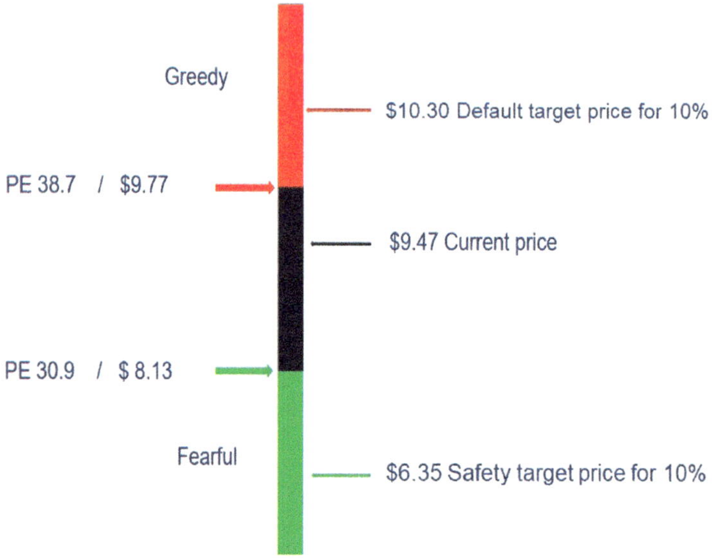

Figure 38—Fear and Greed Indicator

We can now see the ideal buy price of $6.35 sits comfortably in the bottom third of the PE range.

Other Factors to Consider when Buying

Limit orders

Once comfortable with a sensible buy price, we can consider placing a limit order to make the purchase. The advantage of limit orders over market orders is the setting of a guaranteed maximum price rather than an instant purchase at the prevailing price. Limit orders may necessitate waiting for the limit price to be reached, if at all. The purchase order may not be filled under a limit order instruction.

A personal example. Having researched Cochlear for some time, I made one of my happiest purchases in September 2011. My required rate of return could be achieved at a maximum purchase price of $55, compared to the market price of $79 in January 2011. So, I placed an online limit order to automatically activate. Some eight months later, COH made a voluntary recall of its nucleus product which caused fear in the market. The share price tumbled, and my order was filled.

It is almost impossible to pick the bottom of the market, and I remain satisfied with my calculation that $55 represented fair value at the time. The price did continue to fall to a low of $45.11 in this instance, and I could have set an alert as an alternative to a limit order. However, it is emotionally challenging to commit to a purchase when a share price is already falling. Happily, the subsequent years have seen a full recovery and a very healthy capital gain.

Probability

Using the CI methodology does not provide any guarantees, but it does provide the probability of success we seek. There will inevitably be some mistakes in our investment choices, missed opportunities, or things just not going our way. Dr John Price's research reflects that purchasing shares based on the results of the Teaminvest filters will provide us with an 85% probability of a positive outcome over the long term. In other words, a business with a historically strong financial performance leads to a high probability of future success.

In his book *Beating the Street*, Peter Lynch says, 'In the long term, there is a 100% correlation between the success of the company and the success of its stock.'[4]

Over the past 120 years, there has been an 81% probability of a positive return in the Australian share market, showing that the overall trend is already in our favour (see Figure 5).

Despite all the thorough and detailed research that we have undertaken before making a share purchase, we must realise that we can only rely on a *probability* of success. Probability suggests we could be wrong from time to time, so we must learn to accept this as part of the investing journey and be prepared to sell if necessary. Don't allow ego, prejudice, or denial to get in the way. It is no surprise that successful investors such as Lynch, Buffett, and Munger enjoy playing bridge and/or poker noting that probability is what most card games depend on.

Justifying a higher buy price

Technology One is a typical growth business that has come onto the radar of many fund managers. Fund managers are often limited by the businesses they can buy, due to market capitalisation limitations, covenants, and liquidity. Once any business meets their requirements, it will attract the attention of the fund managers who are forever hungry for good growth opportunities. If there is a high conviction in the business, and large parcels of shares are purchased, it will inevitably inflate the share price of the business. Should we, as independent investors in Technology One, confidently believe the current growth of earnings (13.53% per annum) will continue at the same pace—only then may it justify paying above the target price for our own parcel of shares.

Price chart

It's useful here to view a price chart of the entire history of a business to review historical trends/sentiment and how quickly it's recovered from events such as the GFC. Look at the history rationally, not emotionally, and avoid making a hasty purchase for fear of missing out (FOMO).

Too much focus on dividends

At the beginning of this chapter, we discussed the return one could realistically obtain from investing in the share market. Return is made up of both capital gain and dividends. Although dividend yield may appear attractive, especially with franking credits, an element of capital growth should be expected. Telstra's investors were attracted by their 65% average payout ratio over a period of five years, but the lack of growth in earnings was reflected in the share price. Technology One remains a better investment with an average payout ratio of 66% as well as growing earnings, and the benefit of a compounding return.

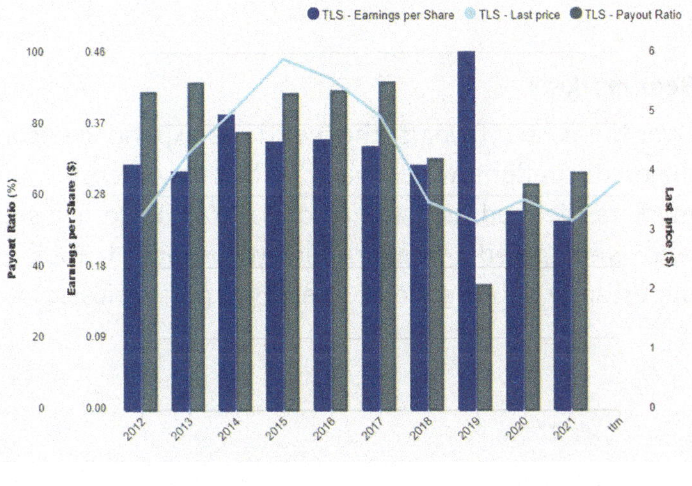

Figure 39—Chart displaying EPS, price, and payout ratio for Telstra

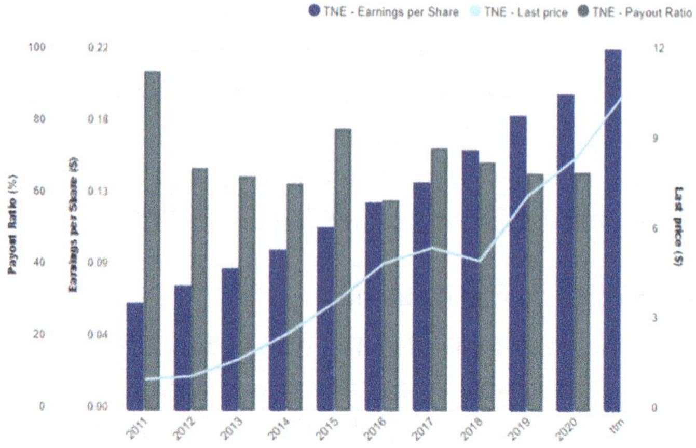

Figure 40—Chart displaying EPS, price, and payout ratio for Technology One

	Capital Gain	Dividends	Total Return
Technology One	14.9%	2.4%	16.3%
Telstra	-5.3%	5.0%	0.3%

Table 7—Showing the capital gain and dividends over the last five years[57]

Bear markets

Over the past 100 years, the world has experienced some major disruptions which has resulted in at least 9 bear markets (defined as a fall of over 20%). Wise investors, who were greedy when others were fearful, took the opportunity to buy good businesses at great prices.

Date	Major events
1914–1918	World War I
September 1929 to June 1932	Wall Street Crash
1939–1945	World War II
7th December 1941	Attack on Pearl Harbour
May 1946 to June 1949	
June 1950	Korean War
December 1961 to June 1962	
November 1968 to May 1970	
January 1973 to October 1974	
November 1955 to April 1975	Vietnam War
November 1980 to August 1982	
August 1987 to December 1987	'Black Monday' financial crash
August 1990–February 1991	The Gulf War
11th September 2001	9/11 terror attack
March 2000 to October 2002	Dot-com bubble
March–December 2003	Second Gulf War
October 2007 to March 2009	Global Financial Crises
23rd June 2016	Brexit
Feb 2020	COVID-19

Table 8—Major world events which affected the share market.[58]
Red indicates the period of a bear market

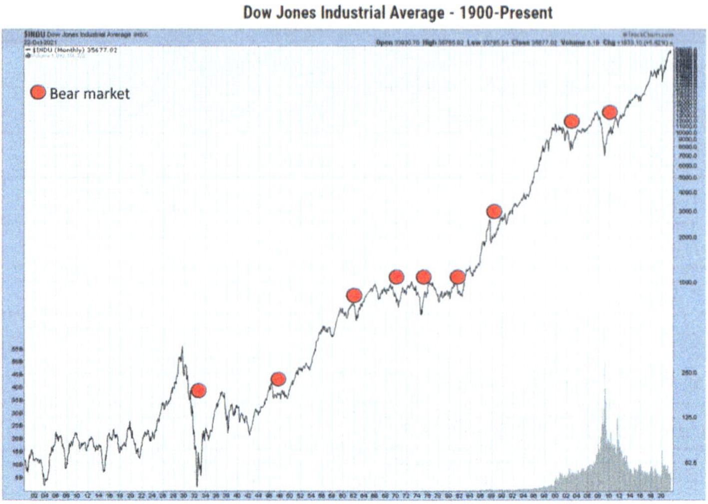

Figure 41—Dow Jones Index over last 80 years[59]

The advent of a bear market creates attractive investment opportunities in businesses we wish to purchase at lower prices. Most often, price drops are simply a result of investor fears, and we can benefit by *embracing* the resulting volatility, as described by Warren Buffet: 'Look at business market fluctuations as your friend rather than your enemy—profit from folly rather than participate in it.' [60]

Diversification

People often wonder how many share investments to hold and why we might suggest an optimum number of 15 to 20. An investor with $100,000 invested into a single business, which subsequently failed, would suffer a 100% loss. Yet, by splitting the capital across two businesses, with one of them failing, the loss is only 50%. One business failing out of three becomes a 33% loss, and so on. The chart below shows there is a dramatic reduction of risk by diversifying, although the effect is less significant once we hold over 15 stocks in a portfolio. Spreading our attention too widely in trying to monitor a large number of businesses could even add to our investing risk.

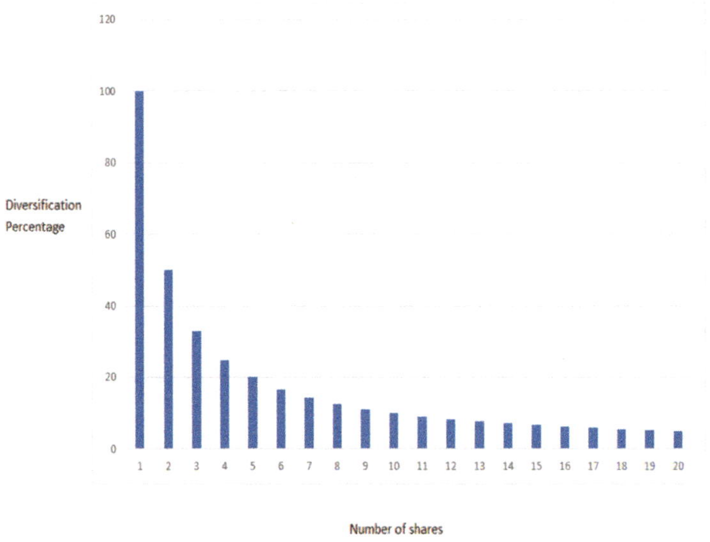

Figure 42—Risk reduction with diversification

This quote from Warren Buffett that describes limiting portfolio size is most appropriate:

> *I could improve your ultimate financial welfare by giving you a ticket with only 20 slots in it so that you had 20 punches—representing all the investments that you got to make in a lifetime. And once you'd punched through the card you couldn't make any more investments at all.*[61]

Chapter Summary

This chapter describes how to establish a sensible buy price or preferable PE. The better-performing businesses that pass steps 1 and 2 will often appear to be too expensive to purchase immediately. This is where patience comes in and we should wait until an opportunity arises, by way of a price drop or correction, so we can purchase shares in premium businesses at a fair price.

Activity: Review the businesses on your watchlist and ascertain what would be a sensible price to pay for them.

Notes

....

....

....

....

....

....

....

....

....

....

....

....

....

....

Part 4

SELLING

Chapter 11
When to Sell

There is so much attention focused on when to buy in the share market, yet hardly any mention of when to sell. Why would that be?

Well, when we think about it, all our conditioning from an early age is around buying. When we buy a car, a house, or even golf clubs, we don't consider when we're likely to sell them. All the advertising we see tells us to buy, buy, buy, and most often now, now, now.

How about when we buy shares in a business? The ideal time to record the criteria and conditions that will be a catalyst for us to sell is when we take the action to buy. If the conditions under which we justify a purchase are no longer valid, then we should consider selling. In addition, when we identify the risks to the continued success of a business, we might annotate the action we'll take should any of these risks subsequently occur; for example, I *will* sell or buy more or hold. Make it simple and straightforward.

Wise words from Peter Lynch: 'Basing a strategy on general maxims, such as "Sell when you double your money" or "cut your losses by selling when the price falls 10%" is absolute folly.' [62]

There are five main flags that may trigger a selling action. Let us explore them further.

The Original Criteria Used are No Longer Valid

At the reporting period, consider selling if the criteria to purchase the stock has changed, for example, a drop in earnings or an increase in debt to equity, for no justifiable reason. If we have owned our shares for some time, we should already be familiar with the business practices.

Fundamentals have Changed

A fundamental change in the direction of the business (for example, overseas expansion) and/or a significant adverse change in the business (for example, departure of CEO).

A Large Acquisition

A large and/or foolish acquisition (may be driven by management ego).

Black Swan Event

An unpredictable 'black swan' event, such as the COVID pandemic, whereby businesses (for example, travel) have been affected.[63]

Better Opportunity Elsewhere

If we believe there is a better growth opportunity for our capital in a different business or type of investment.

'Sell a stock because the business's fundamentals deteriorate, not because the sky is falling'.[64]

Profit-taking

Some investors decide to take profits when their investment has grown significantly in capital value. There are several considerations with this approach:

- Where to place the funds while waiting to reinvest, especially in a low interest rate environment.
- Investing in a lesser-known business with lower prospects of matching earlier gains.
- Missing the opportunity for compounding of capital gains.
- Dismissing all the time and effort taken to conduct the initial and ongoing research, attending AGMs, and so on.
- Capital gains tax implications.

A fellow investor bought CSL shares in Aug 2011 for $27.60. He sold them eighteen months later, at $55.80 to 'realise' the 100% gain. Today as I write, CSL shares are trading at $338.31. He has since acknowledged that he unwisely sold purely on price movement.

Tip Be wary of becoming emotionally attached to an investment (they are not children or pets!).

When the share price drops, we suffer from loss aversion bias and instinctively feel that everyone is selling, when it may only be a small percentage of investors. For example, the Technology One current average daily transactions of around 740k equates to just 0.2% of 371.8 million shares on offer. The remaining 99.8% of investors are passive.

Directors are legally obligated to disclose anything that could impact on share price, both positively and negatively. Should an unexplained drop in share price occur, it may well be due to rumours and not a reason to immediately sell.

Our past success at work or in business may not automatically translate well into success in the share market, as opposing strategies are often required. For example, perseverance is considered a desirable trait when running a business, yet the same trait can be a disadvantage when holding onto a losing investment. Be committed to act on your selling criteria when the time comes.

I will add one more reason you may decide to sell. An investor told me she placed a limit order to buy 1,000 Pro Medicus® shares at a limit order of $32, filled on 12 January 2021. A few days later, she celebrated, on seeing her shares surge by 25% on the back of a new positive contract. She then discovered she had, in fact, erroneously purchased 10,000 shares instead of 1,000 and had made a gain of nearly $80,000 in 3 days. She decided to sell the excess shares immediately and make the most out of her 'good' mistake!

Chapter Summary

This chapter introduced the concept of being more conditioned to buying rather than selling. A predetermined trigger is very helpful here to avoid hesitancy or denial which could result in taking no action at all.

Activity: Refer to the buying criteria recorded for each business in your portfolio and annotate what must change to justify selling. Take into consideration the risks previously identified with each business. A price fall is not one of them!

Notes

....

....

....

....

....

....

....

....

....

....

....

....

....

....

....

....

....

....

Part 5

SUMMARY

Chapter 12
Bringing it all Together

Congratulations on working through the material presented in this book. I trust I have provided you with a solid framework, meaningful principles, and a logical process to follow in order to select some great businesses to invest in.

Hopefully, you now appreciate why the book began with your mindset, as it has become integral to every chapter thereafter. The progression into biases was designed to make you aware of the pitfalls that investors can inadvertently fall victim to. I devoted a good part of the content to becoming familiar with assessing financial statements and understanding ratios. The more this is used in practice, the more exponential the benefit will be. The templates I have used from ARB have provided practical examples and, as they will become outdated, the **<www.teaminvest.com.au/how-to-use-conscious-investor>** website will be updated twice a year with the latest financials.

Human interactions are central to our lives, and I hope that your active participation at AGMs and visiting business sites, as part of your research into worthy management, will become intuitive over time. The idea of moats and risks is not new as we instinctively look for unique benefits in addition to the potential downsides of any major investment we make.

My personal conviction remains strong in the methodology I have shared with you. While I fully appreciate the steps advocated within these pages may not be the only way to profit from the share market, I am immensely confident in the 3 steps described and the process employed to achieve a level of investment success.

- Step 1—filtering the numbers to find financially sound businesses.
- Step 2—exploring in detail the business activities and the people in charge.
- Step 3—buying shares in approved businesses at a sensible price.

This is by no means the end of the story as the monitoring process should keep you engaged with the businesses in your portfolio. In the event that a significant risk to a business has been identified, you'll hopefully follow your predetermined action plan in order to sell your holdings. As we have discussed, selling is counterintuitive to many people, so a clearly articulated action plan becomes invaluable at this stage.

My goal for this book has been to impart some of my own passion for investing while providing useful techniques to make the investing process easier and more rewarding.

Feel free to test any aspects covered in this book and embrace the learning experience.

The process discussed should equip you with a good probability of success and I wish you great enjoyment and financial gain in your own investing journey.

Happy investing!

Appendix 1
Financial Statements and Explanations

The three main financial statements are the balance sheet, profit and loss or income statement, and cash flow statement.

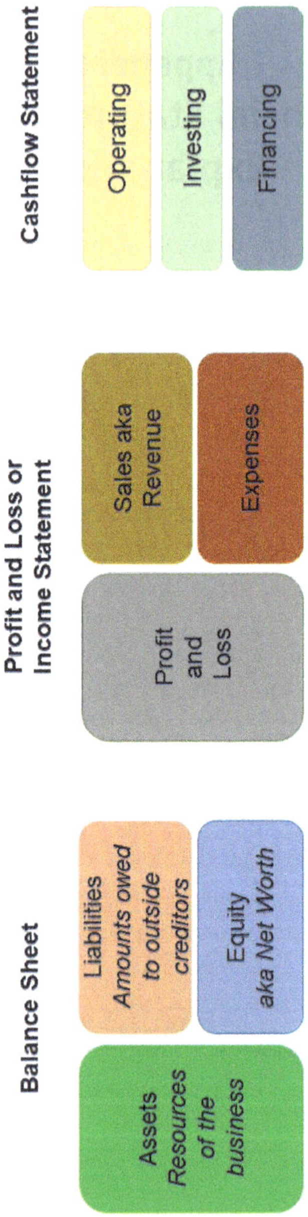

Figure 43—The key components of the financial statements

- The balance sheet reflects a business's financial position (assets, liabilities, and equity). It is a snapshot of these positions at the end of the reporting period or a point in time.
- The profit and loss (or income statement) details how much money has been made or lost during the reporting period. This is all the business has made selling its products and services, less the expenditure on manufacturing and delivering those products and services. The result is the income, also known as earnings or profits.
- The cash flow statement reflects what cash has come into and out of the business during the reporting period.

To obtain a free copy of these statements and 6-monthly updates, please go to **<www.teaminvest.com.au/how-to-use-conscious-investor>**.

Let's now look at the three main accounting statements of ARB in turn.

BALANCE SHEET STATEMENT

Current assets (less than 12 months)
Non-current assets

Total assets

Current liabilities (less than 12 months)
Non-current liabilities

Total liabilities

NET ASSETS

TOTAL EQUITY

Total Assets - Total Liabilities = Net Assets (Equity)

Figure 44—Key components of a balance sheet

BALANCE SHEET STATEMENT 2021	$'000
Current assets	
Cash and cash equivalents	84,771
Receivables	79,890
Derivative financial instruments	151
Inventories	172,958
Other assets	6,292
Total current assets	**344,062**
Non-current assets	
Property, plant and equipment	201,434
Deferred tax assets	9,977
Intangible assets	63,110
Right-of-use	39,679
Total non-current assets	**314,200**
Total assets	**658,262**
Current liabilities	
Payables	73,234
Derivative financial instruments	74
Borrowings	
Current tax liabilities	14,168
Lease liabilities	5,927
Provisions	19,414
Total current liabilities	**112,817**
Non-current liabilities	
Lease liabilities	39,200
Deferred tax liabilities	933
Provisions	19,535
Total non-current liabilities	**59,668**
Total liabilities	**172,485**
NET ASSETS	**485,777**
EQUITY	
Contributed equity	170,789
Reserves	9,522
Retained earnings	305,466
TOTAL EQUITY	**485,777**

Figure 45—Detailed view of ARB's balance sheet

PROFIT AND LOSS STATEMENT

Sales / Revenue	aka 'Top line'. Note: It is important to understand how the revenue is recognised i.e. upfront or over time.
- Cost of Goods	(COGS) Costs mainly for material & labour making the product or delivering the service. Also includes change in inventory. Mainly direct costs and some overhead allocation
= Gross Profit	aka Gross Income
- Expenses	S,G & A' (Selling, General & Adminstration) expenses. Money spent to develop, sell or account for the product and manage the making and selling process. Overheads which are incurred with the running of the business that cannot be directly related to the cost of making or purchasing the things the business sells
= Earnings before Tax, Interest, Depreciation and Amo	(EBITDA) Operating income
- Depreciation and amortisation expense	
= Earnings Before Income Tax and Interest	(EBIT)
- Interest expense	
= Earnings before Tax	EBT aka PBT (Profit before Tax)
- Income tax expense	
= Net Profit after Tax	(NPAT) Reported or Statutory or Operating earnings
- / + Abnormal or Extraordinary items	i.e. Acquistion costs, write offs or downs
= Net Profit After Tax and Abnormals	(NPAT) aka 'Bottom line', Normalised or Underlying

Basic earnings = earnings / o/s equity shares of the company (outstanding common shares)
Diluted earnings = earnings / all shares (options etc) Present a clearer picture of EPS
Statutory profit = the earnings that standard accounting practices require a company to report on its income statement
Statutory figures are those presented by the company in their formal company reports & include all items that affect the earnings & are auditec

Figure 46—High-level view of the key sections of the profit and loss statement

PROFIT AND LOSS STATEMENT	**2021 $'000**
Sales revenue	623,072
Other income	2,785
Total revenue and other income	**625,857**
Materials and consumables used	(278,878)
Employee expenses	(129,093)
Government wage subsidies	9,819
Depreciation and amortisation expense	(23,513)
Advertising expenses	(5,975)
Distribution expenses	(14,467)
Finance expenses	(2,002)
Occupancy expenses	(13,820)
Maintenance expenses	(5,065)
Other expenses	(12,840)
Profit before income tax expenses	**150,023**
Income tax expenses	(37,128)
Profit attributable to members of the parent entity	**112,895**
Basic and Diluted Earnings per share (cents)	**140.0**

Figure 47—Profit and Loss Statement of ARB

Payout Ratio (PO)	✓ Dividends / Earnings ✓ Benchmark > 50% ✓ 54,991 / 112,895 = 48.6%
Earnings per share (EPS)	✓ Earnings / # of shares ✓ Benchmark: growing over the past 5 years ✓ 112,895 / 80.66 = 1.40c
Sales per share (SPS)	✓ Revenue / # of shares ✓ Benchmark: growing over past 5 years ✓ 623,072 / 81.5 = 7.642c
Net Profit Margin (NPM)	✓ Earnings / Sales ✓ Benchmark: steady / growing over past 5 yrs ✓ 112,895 / 623,072 = 18.1%

** Morningstar has correctly used the weighted average number of shares 80.66m – See note 25. For SPS, 81.5m shares were used. This inconsistency is not material as ARB has issued relatively few shares but would be material where a company has a large cash issue as SPS would then be understated.*

Table 9—The key financial ratios derived from the profit and loss statement and balance sheet

Cash Flow Statement

The cash flow statement records cash coming into and out of the business. It reveals exactly how the cash is being spent and how financially sound the business is. In addition, it shows how well a business manages cash and pays off debts, and how well it can meet operating expenses.

The cash flow statement is different from the profit and loss statement, which includes any inflows and outflows that are recorded on credit as opposed to cash.

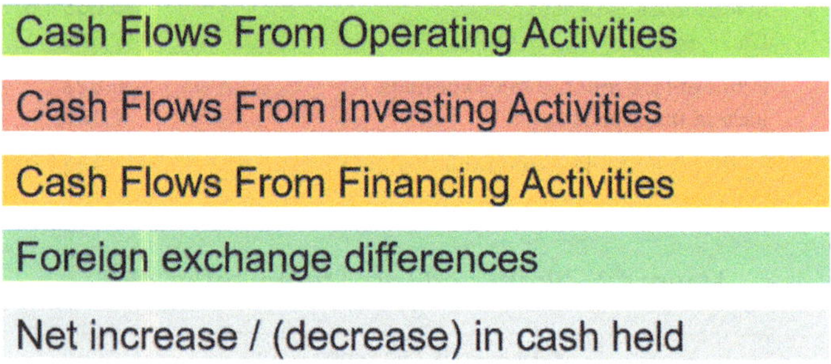

Figure 48—High-level view of the cash flow statement

The cash flow statement is broken into three parts:

- Operating Activities
  - Shows how much cash is generated from the operations of the business, which will include any cash sales, interest payments, and payments to suppliers and employees.
  - Non-cash items are not included in the cash flow statement. These are revealed in the profit and loss statement and assets and liabilities are reflected in the balance sheet.

- Investing Activities
  - Investing activities include any business investments; the most common investment would be in purchasing assets such as machinery, plant and equipment, property, and so on.
  - It makes sense for a business to invest excess cash sitting on the books. For example, an insurance business receives premiums upfront so it would be wise to invest these funds until they are required to settle claims.
- Financing Activities
  - A typical example is payments for dividends and borrowings.

CASHFLOW STATEMENT	**2021 $'000**
Cash Flows From Operating Activities	
Receipts from customers	651,141
Payments to suppliers and employees	(516,480)
Interest received	151
Finance costs	(1,864)
Income tax paid	(29,777)
Net cash provided by Operating activities	**103,171**
Cash Flows From Investing Activities	
Payments for property, plant and equipment	(33,138)
Payments for development costs	(2,754)
Payments for intangible software assets	(711)
Proceeds from sales of property, plant & equipment	783
Payments for business acquisition	(15,188)
Net cash used in Investing activities	**(51,008)**
Cash Flows From Financing Activities	
Dividends paid	
Payments for lease liabilities	(551)
Proceeds from borrowings	(5,399)
Repayment of borrowings	(3,391)
Net cash used in Financing activities	**(9,341)**
Foreign exchange differences	380
Net increase / (decrease) in cash held	**43,202**
Cash at the beginning of the financial year	41,569
Cash at the end of the financial year	84,771

Figure 49—Cash flow statement of ARB

Free Cashflow	✓ Operating cashflow – net capital expenditure ✓ 103,171 – 35,820 (33,138 + 2,754 + 711 – 783) = 67,351
Operating Cashflow	✓ Net cash from Operating activities ✓ 103,171

Table 10—Key ratios from the cash flow statement of ARB

	2021
Operating Cash Flow	103,171
Net capital expenditure	-35,820
Free Cashflow	67,351
Less Payments for business acquisitions	-15,188
Less dividends paid*	0
Less other net cash used in financing activities	-9,341
Plus Foreign exchange differences	380
Payment for lease liabilities	0
	-24,149
Net change in cash	43,202
Opening cash	41,569
Closing cash	84,771
	(43,202)

* Some readers may wonder why there is no cash outflow from dividends when some $54,000 was "paid out' in dividends in FY 2021. The explanation seems to lie with the new shares issued to the underwriters of the company's DRP scheme. See Consolidated Statement of Changes in Equity. In effect dividends were funded entirely by issuing new shares.

Figure 50—Breakdown of ARB's cash flow

Tip

A cash flow statement provides a transparent and essential assessment of the business and will show how well it can meet its future expenses. A business will be in a better position, the more cash it has on hand.

Bringing it all together. Using all the tables covered in this Appendix, the investor should be able to crosscheck ARB's actual financial statements with each financial ratio and how they are derived. The key components are highlighted with a red outline. Using ROE (return on equity) as an example, we can see from Table 11, the earnings are divided by the equity (Assets – Liabilities {Book value}) and the figures of these components are:

112,895 / 485,777 = 23.2%, as highlighted in Figures 45 and 47.

Management	6/2012	6/2013	6/2014	6/2015	6/2016	6/2017	6/2018	6/2019	6/2020	6/2021		
ROE %	25.5	23.9	21.5	19.5	19.0	18.1	16.8	16.5	15.4	23.2		
ROC %	25.5	23.9	21.5	19.6	19.1	18.1	16.9	16.5	14.2	21.8		
Growth	**6/2012**	**6/2013**	**6/2014**	**6/2015**	**6/2016**	**6/2017**	**6/2018**	**6/2019**	**6/2020**	**6/2021**	**EPSttm**	**HGROWTH**
EPS $	0.531	0.584	0.587	0.578	0.599	0.621	0.643	0.719	0.718	1.40	1.40	14.2%
SPS $	3.707	4.022	4.108	4.166	4.508	4.832	5.344	5.568	5.830	7.642		9.5%
Debt	**6/2012**	**6/2013**	**6/2014**	**6/2015**	**6/2016**	**6/2017**	**6/2018**	**6/2019**	**6/2020**	**6/2021**		
DEq%	0.0	0.0	0.0	0.9	0.0	0.0	1.3	0.0	12.0	9.3		
DMCap	0.0	0.0	0.0	0.2	0.0	0.0	0.3	0.0	3.2	1.7		
Debt payback	0.0	0.0	0.0	0.0	0.0	0.0	0.1	0.0	0.8	0.4		
Liquidity	**6/2012**	**6/2013**	**6/2014**	**6/2015**	**6/2016**	**6/2017**	**6/2018**	**6/2019**	**6/2020**	**6/2021**		
IC	0.0	0.0	0.0	100.00	100.00	100.00	100.00	100.00	46.3	75.9		
CR	3.3	3.4	3.5	3.1	3.6	3.4	2.9	3.8	3.1	3.0		
QR	1.9	2.0	1.8	1.2	1.4	1.6	1.1	1.3	1.4	1.5		
Payout	**6/2012**	**6/2013**	**6/2014**	**6/2015**	**6/2016**	**6/2017**	**6/2018**	**6/2019**	**6/2020**	**6/2021**		
Payout %	47.1	47.9	49.4	223.2	52.6	54.8	57.5	55.0	55.0	48.6		
NPM	**6/2012**	**6/2013**	**6/2014**	**6/2015**	**6/2016**	**6/2017**	**6/2018**	**6/2019**	**6/2020**	**6/2021**		
NPM %	14.3	14.5	14.3	13.4	13.3	12.8	12.0	12.9	12.3	18.1		
P/E and Price	**6/2012**	**6/2013**	**6/2014**	**6/2015**	**6/2016**	**6/2017**	**6/2018**	**6/2019**	**6/2020**	**6/2021**	**TTM**	**Current**
P/E High	18.2	23.6	23.6	25.1	28.4	29.8	37.2	32.5	28.8	34.0	38.9	36.0
P/E Low	12.5	15.3	17.8	18.1	20.9	23.0	23.3	20.3	14.5	12.6	19.7	
Price high	9.65	13.82	13.88	14.49	17.00	18.50	23.94	23.32	20.64	47.58	54.46	50.46
Price low	6.65	8.93	10.46	10.49	12.52	14.28	14.99	14.55	10.40	17.68	27.62	
Company size	**6/2012**	**6/2013**	**6/2014**	**6/2015**	**6/2016**	**6/2017**	**6/2018**	**6/2019**	**6/2020**	**6/2021**		
Shares M	72.5	72.5	72.5	79.2	79.2	79.2	79.3	79.7	79.8	81.5		
Earnings	**6/2012**	**6/2013**	**6/2014**	**6/2015**	**6/2016**	**6/2017**	**6/2018**	**6/2019**	**6/2020**	**6/2021**		
Earnings $M	38.5	42.4	42.6	44.1	47.4	49.2	51.0	57.1	57.3	112.9		
Sales $M	268.7	291.5	297.8	329.8	356.9	382.6	424.0	443.9	465.4	623.1		

Table 11—Key Financial Ratios and how their calculations are derived

			Benchmark
Earnings per Share	EPS	Earnings / Shares on Offer 112,895 / 80.66 = $140.0	Growing each year by at least 3%
Sales per Share	SPS	Sales / Shares on offer 623,072 / 81.5 = $7.64	Growing each year by at least 3%
Net Profit Margin	NPM	Earnings / Sales 112,895 / 623,072 = 18.1%	Consistent and growing
Interest Cover	IC	Earnings before tax / Expenses (Interest related) 152,025 (150,023 + 2,002) / 2,002 = 75.9	Higher than 5
Market Capitilisation	MCap	Shares on offer x Price 81,533,865 x $43.19 = $3.52b	Higher than $100m
Payout Ratio	PO	Dividends / Earnings 54,991 (23,193 + 31,798) / 112,895 = 48.6%	Higher than 40%
Return on Capital	ROC	Earnings / Equity + Long term Debt 112,895 - (2,002 x 0.7) / 485,777 + 39,200) = 21.8%	Higher than 10%
Return on Equity	ROE	Earnings / Equity (Assets - Liabilities {Book value}) 112,895 / 485,777 = 23.2%	Higher than 10%
Debt to Equity	D/Eq	Debt / Equity 45,127 (39,200 + 5,927) / 485,777 = 9.3%	Lower than 50%
Current Ratio	CR	Current Assets / Current Liabilities 344,062 / 112,817 = 3.0	Higher than 1.25
Quick Ratio	QR	Current Assets less inventory / Equity 164,661 (84,771 + 79,890) / 112,817 = 1.5	Higher than 0.75
PE / EPS Growth	PEG	PE / EPS Growth 36 / 14.2 = 2.5	Less than 1

Table 12—ARB's financials as per CI

Appendix 2
Annual Report

Although formats can vary, annual reports are often boilerplate which makes them increasingly familiar the more you read. It might be helpful to look up the business websites and/or <www.asx.com.au> and download the business's presentations. They provide a particularly good high-level insight into the business and an easy introduction to their activities. Due to COVID, it's becoming more popular to listen to the business AGM online. Whilst this is certainly more convenient, it does mean we will miss the wonderful ability to assess the board and management in person and the opportunity to mingle after the meeting.

Format of a Typical Annual Report

- Chairman's report
- CEO or MD report
- Remuneration report
- Finance reports
- Profit and loss
- Balance sheet
- Cash flow statement
- Director's declaration
- Notes to the finances
- Audit report
- Corporate governance statement
- Environmental, social, and governance report.

The length of the report will vary with the size and complexity of the business.

I recommend starting by downloading the ARB annual report as an easy report to follow and understand.

Appendix 3
Checklist

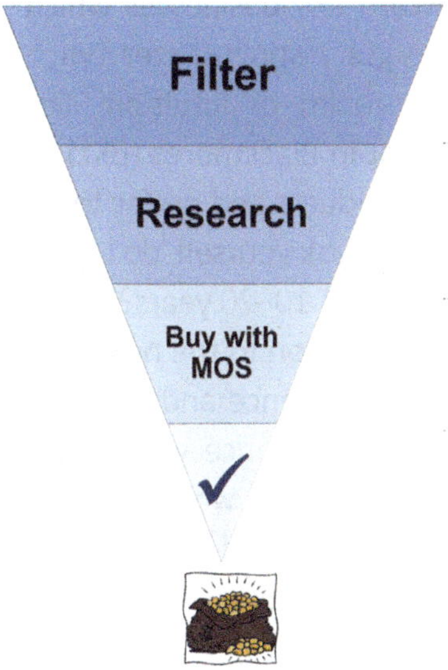

- *Step 1: Quantitative filter on key financial metrics.*
- *Step 2: Qualitative assessment of the management, the business and its moats and risks*
- *Step 3: Determine a fair purchase price with a Margin Of Safety.*
- *Be patient until the investment becomes available*

Figure 51—The three steps

Like any good pilot, I refer to a checklist for my flying, and I created one for share investing, too.

Step 1: Quantitative Filtering

a. Apply the CI scanning tool to filter the share market to find financially sound businesses. The main criteria over at least a five-year period are:
    - Return on equity > 10%
    - Return on capital > 10%

- Debt to equity < 50%
- Sales per share growing > 3%
- Earnings per share growing > 3%
- Current ratio > 1.25
- Quick ratio > 0.75
- Interest cover > 5.

b. From the resulting list, discard any businesses which don't satisfy an immediate gut instinct. Peter Lynch refers to this as 'art—the realm of intuition'. For example, I prefer not to invest in Blackmores (BKL) as I simply don't believe in its products and prefer to be congruent. Look at your list and ask yourself 'do I think this business will still be around in 10–20 years?' If the answer is not a definite *yes*, move on to the next one. Stick to your own circle of competence and comfort. Staying within our circle of competence will ensure we fully understand the business in which we are investing. Buffett muses, 'If we can't find things within our circle of competence, we don't expand the circle. We'll wait.'[65]

Step 2: Qualitative Filtering

Read at least the last two annual and interim reports.

Items to focus on in the reports:

- Chairman and CEO reports. Compare their comments from the previous year. Is there consistency? Do they make excuses? Is the CEO's strategy clear?
- Board/Management—what is the members' tenure on the board? Other positions held? How are they remunerated and what are their hurdle rates? How many shares do they hold?
- What is the business's noble purpose?

- How does it make money? What is its outlook?
- Read the notes to the financials—anything untoward?
- While reading the report, think about the business moats (areas to consider: legislative, geographic, patent or technology, long-term contractual, price or costs, process or people, distribution channel, trap door) and for each one ascertain both their depth and durability.
- For each moat, there will be an associated risk (areas to consider):
    - **Non-Business**: sovereign, political, economic, regulatory, environmental, social, technological change, disruptive competition
    - **Business**: brand, sector, changes in technology, irrational competition, changes in CEO or executive management, erosion of moats, reputation
    - **Financials**: Is there anything about the financials that worries you?
- Think about the likelihood of each risk occurring, and if it did, what damage it would have on the business. Make a log of what you would do if a risk does occur—will you sell, buy more, or hold?

Look up the past six months of announcements, read the CEO's presentation to analysts (available on Listcorp and the ASX website) to get a quick overview.

Step 3: Purchase Price

Ideally, we want to buy a business when it is in the bottom third of its 4-year PE range and meets your required rate of return in CI. Compare the business PE to its industry, and the market as a whole, to glean what is fair value. Determine your buy price and set it as a limit order.

Appendix 4
A History of Conscious Investor® by John Price

It started while I was living in the US. I had moved there in 1990 to become head of the mathematics department of a small international university. My primary area of research was financial mathematics, an arcane area with particular applications to helping large corporations manage future risks associated with interest rates, asset prices, and exchange rates.

At the same time, I started giving presentations on the importance of investing in companies with products and services you believed in and possibly used. In this way, you favoured companies that contributed to the type of country or environment you wanted to live in. I called this being a conscious investor.

By chance, I attended an annual meeting of Berkshire Hathaway. When Warren Buffett started talking, I was hooked. It made so much sense. Particularly when it was backed up by the penetrating comments by Charlie Munger.

At the meeting, I made up my mind to treat Buffett as a research project by getting hold of as much as possible of what he had said and written. (I describe my experience of the meeting in 'The Day I Became a Buffetteer' in *Finding Wealth Winners® the Teaminvest Way* (*FWTW*).)

My first goal was to understand his methods. My second goal was to put this into a software package so that I could put them into practice. When people heard about this, they wanted a copy of the software. This necessitated it being put into a form that could be used by any diligent investor. The software became what is now called Conscious Investor®.

Over time, I developed several key principles. Some of these principles were already known, but I found they were generally only described in a confused manner. So, I rewrote them. Others were developed from scratch, are original, and are unique.

In some cases, once the principle was established, completely new methods and functions had to be developed to implement it. This was because nothing appropriate was available in the existing investment software or literature.

As an example, the foundational principle I developed for Conscious Investor is based on the fundamental question for an investor: what rate of return can I be confident of achieving? This is quite different from the usual valuation methods which are based on calculating intrinsic value using discounted cash flow (DCF) methods.

As a mathematician, I knew that while the DCF method is a fine abstract academic theory, it is deceptive if applied to real companies. For instance, minute changes in input variables can lead to changes of orders of magnitude in the outcome. Also, it contains the impossible assumption of forecasts of interest rates out to infinity.

To implement the return principle, I developed two new functions, STRET® and STRETD®. The first function calculates future return, the second future return assuming dividends are reinvested. Another key new function is STAEGR® which measures the level of stability of the past growth of earnings. My research showed when STAEGR was high, the future growth of earnings per share tended to be similar to the past growth. Having confidence in this future growth was vital for locating Wealth Winners® using STRET and STRETD.

In other cases, once the principle was established, rather than developing new functions, it was necessary to develop new high-level functionality. For example, the overall functionality of *Filter, Research* and *Return* in Conscious Investor provides an inclusive map for users.

Another unique set of principles were constructed around the idea of margins of safety. These are built-in stress-testing procedures to help ensure that even when future business and market conditions are less favourable, the performance still exceeds the requirements for a satisfactory investment. The margins of safety functions operate in the areas of business growth, general market opinion, and board actions.

As the principles were developed, I subjected them to a gruelling testing process. Did they make sense? Were there any hidden complications? What happens under extreme market conditions? Were they intuitive and easy to apply? Did they add to the performance? Did the principles build on each other and work together harmoniously? (You can see more details in 'Origins, Principles and Functions of Conscious Investor: Parts A and B' in *FWTW*.)

Appendix 5
Recommended Websites and Books

There are many books on share investing and financial literacy as well as a multitude of excellent online or formal courses. Listed below are some websites I refer to and some favourite books in my personal library.

www.teaminvest.com.au	www.asx.com.au
www.belldirect.com.au	www.theinvestorspodcast.com
www.commsec.com.au	www.stockdoctor.com.au
www.listcorp.com.au	www.investopedia.com
www.stockopedia.com	www.sharesight.com.au

A Honnold, *Alone on The Wall*, Pan, 2015.

R Mason, *Chickenhawk,* RandomHouse UK, London, 1984 (Had to include that, to learn more about helicopters).

KL Fisher, *Common Stocks and Uncommon Profits,* John Wiley & Sons Inc, New York, 1996.

JC Bogle, *Enough,* John Wiley & Sons Inc, Hoboken, 2010.

H Rosling, *Factfulness,* Hodder & Stoughton, London, 2018.

D Gardner, *Future Babble: Why Expert Predictions Fail - and Why We Believe Them Anyway,* Plume, New York, 2011.

K Fisher, *Markets Never Forget,* John Wiley & Sons Inc, Hoboken, 2011.

P Lynch, *One Up on Wall Street,* Simon & Schuster UK, London, 2000.

W Green, *Richer, Wiser Happier,* Scribner, New York, 2021.

R Pape, *The Barefoot Investor,* John Wiley & Sons Australia, Milton, 2020.

B Lev and F Gu, *The End of Accounting and the Path Forward for Investors and Managers,* John Wiley & Sons Inc, Hoboken, 2016.

C Zook and J Allen, *The Founder's Mentality,* Harvard Business Review Publishing, Brighton, 2016.

J Greenblatt, *The Little Book that Still Beats the Market,* John Wiley & Sons Inc, Hoboken, 2006.

C Nicholson, *The Psychology of Investing,* Wilkinson Publishing, Melbourne, 2006.

J O'Loughlin, *The Real Warren Buffett: Managing Capital, Leading People,* Nicholas Brealey Publishing, 2004.

D Krueger, *The Secret Language of Money,* McGraw-Hill, New York, 2009.

RG Hagstrom, *The Warren Buffett Way,* John Wiley & Sons, Hoboken, 2004.

D Kahneman, *Thinking, Fast and Slow,* Random House, 2011.

M Buffet and D, *Warren Buffett and the Interpretation of Financial Statements,* Simon & Schuster UK, London, 2011.

J Lowe, *Warren Buffett Speaks,* John Wiley & Sons, Hoboken, 2007.

J Zweig, *Your Money & Your Brain,* Simon & Schuster US, New York, 2007.

H Coleman and Dr J Price, *Finding Wealth Winners the Teaminvest Way,* self published, 2020.

Dr J Price, *The Conscious Investor,* John Wiley & Sons, 2011.

Glossary

All Ordinaries index (XAO) The top 500 businesses by market capitalisation listed on the Australian Share Market make up the All-Ordinaries Index. Currently, there are 2,288 businesses listed on the stock exchange.

Covenants When loans are made, contracts are drawn up and there are certain arrangements and obligations associated with payments terms, time, and so on. Sometimes the lender may face restrictions on what they can do with the money, known as covenants.

EBITDA Earnings before interest, taxes, depreciation, and amortisation.

Moat Something unique about the business. A point of difference. A sustainable competitive advantage over its competitors.

NPAT Net profit after tax.

Net profit margin Net profit divided by net sales.

VIX The Chicago Board Options Exchange Volatility Index is referred to by stock and options traders to gauge the market's anxiety level. Put simply, it is a mathematical measure of how much the market thinks the S&P 500 Index option, or SPX, will fluctuate over the next 12 months, based upon an analysis of the difference between current SPX put and call option prices. Although the VIX isn't expressed as a percentage, it could be understood as one. A VIX of 22 translates to implied volatility of 22% on the SPX. It means the index has a 66.7% probability (being one standard deviation, statistically speaking) of trading within a range 22% higher than—or lower than—its current level, over the next year. The VIX rises when *put* option buying increases, and falls when *call* buying activity is more robust. (Note: A put option gives the purchaser the right—but not the obligation—to sell a security for a specified price by a certain time. A call option is a right to buy the same.)[66]

Working capital The capital required to run the daily affairs of the business, which is a measure of its liquidity. It is defined as the difference between a business's current assets and current liabilities.

List of References

1. Forbes Media LLC, 'Top 10 Life Lessons from Warren Buffett', 4 Oct 2015, viewed 23 Nov 2021, https://www.forbes.com/pictures/eede45imgh/there-seems-to-be-some-p/#1a6a63783f86.
2. CNBC LLC, 'Charlie Munger praises this 1 trait of Warren Buffett's without it, "you won't get very far in life"', 21 April 2019, viewed 23 Nov 2021, https://www.cnbc.com/2019/04/21/billionaire-charlie-munger-praises-this-1-skill-of-warren-buffetts-without-it-you-wont-get-very-far-in-life.html.
3. PD Kaufman (Ed), *Poor Charlie's Almanack*, Walsworth Publishing, Missouri, 2005, p 393.
4. P Lynch, *Beating the Street*, Simon and Schuster UK, London, 1994.
5. W Buffet, Chairman's Letter to Shareholders, 29 Feb 1988, viewed 23 Nov 2021, Berkshire Hathaway, https://www.berkshirehathaway.com/letters/letters.html.
6. B Graham, *The Intelligent Investor*, HarperCollins, New York, 2003.
7. Nasdaq Inc, 'The Greatest Mathematical Discovery of all Time', Investing Answers, 8 Jul 2010, viewed 23 Nov 2021, The Greatest Mathematical Discovery of All Time | Nasdaq.
8. J Metacreator, 'On Opinions and Mental Discipline', *john metacreator trying to win the metaverse* [web blog], 22

Nov 2019, viewed 23 Nov 2021, https://john.do/opinions-mental-discipline/.
9. Marketwatch Inc, CBOE Volatility Index, *Marketwatch*, 2021, viewed 23 Nov 2021, https://www.marketwatch.com/investing/index/vix/charts?mod=mw_quote_advanced.
10. J Price, *The Conscious Investor,* John Wiley & Sons Inc (US), New Jersey, 2010.
11. M Mullenweg, 'Adam Robinson on Understanding', *Asides*, 22 Nov 2017, viewed 23 Nov 2021, https://ma.tt/2017/11/adam-robinson-on-understanding/.
12. Quote Investigator, 'Everything Should Be Made as Simple as Possible, But Not Simpler', 13 May 2011, viewed 23 Nov 2021, Everything Should Be Made as Simple as Possible, But Not Simpler – Quote Investigator.
13. CNBC LLC, 'Billionaire Investor Warren Buffett on CNBC's "Squawk Box"', *CNBC Excerpts,* 2 Mar 2015, viewed 23 Nov 2021 https://www.cnbc.com/2015/03/02/cnbc-excerpts-billionaire-investor-warren-buffett-on-cnbcs-squawk-box-today.html.
14. M Buffett and D Clark, *The Tao of Warren Buffett*, Simon & Schuster UK, London, 2009.
15. Market Index Pty Ltd, 'Market Statistics', 2021, viewed 23 Nov 2021, Market Statistics (ASX): PE, Earnings & Yield - Market Index.

Note: Historical returns are based on the All-Ordinaries Accumulation Index (XAOAI), which includes dividends. The All Ordinaries (XAO) was first published in 1980 with a starting value of 500. The index tracks the 500 largest companies on the Australian share market and is weighted by market capitalisation (so large companies have a greater effect on the index movement). The All-Ordinaries Accumulation Index (XAOAI) was created at the same time with a starting value of 1,000. The XAOAI is identical to the XAO except it includes dividends in its calculation. Data before 1980 is inconsistent between sources and should not be relied upon for investment purposes. Regional indices from 1900–1979 used different methodologies to record share price index movements. All studies and historical index statistics analysed by the editor of Market Index were strongly correlated but never identical. Only data from 1990 onwards can be verified by the editor of Market Index.

Original concept by AXA ("109 years of Australian share market returns"). Linkable source no longer published online.

16. Andex Charts, www.andex.com.au.
17. FMR LLC, 'Lessons from an investing legend', *Fidelity Viewpoints,* 8 Nov 2021, viewed 23 Nov 2021, https://www.fidelity.com/viewpoints/investing-ideas/peter-lynch-investment-strategy.
18. Conscious Investor, COCHLEAR LIMITED, Research, Data, https://online.consciousinvestor.com/.
19. Conscious Investor, ARB LIMITED, Research, Data, https://online.consciousinvestor.com/.
20. Codan Limited, *2014 Codan Annual Report*, n.d., viewed 23 Nov 2021, https://codan.com.au/site-content/uploads/2017/04/2014_Codan-Annual-Report.pdf.
21. Conscious Investor, CODAN, Research, Growth chart, https://online.consciousinvestor.com/.
22. Conscious Investor, FISHER & PAYKEL, Research, Growth, charts, https://online.consciousinvestor.com/.
23. Conscious Investor, ARB CORPORATION LIMITED, Research, Data, https://online.consciousinvestor.com/.
24. Conscious Investor, CSL, Research, Data, https://online.consciousinvestor.com/.

25. GEO Investing, 'A Gem of a Video Discovery on Lynch's Stock Picking Process', *Stock Shop with Peter Lynch*, 2 Dec 2019, viewed 23 Nov 2021, https://geoinvesting.com/peter-lynch-stock-picking-process/.
26. Conscious Investor, ARB CORPORATION LIMITED, Research, Charts, https://online.consciousinvestor.com/.
27. Conscious Investor, TECHNOLOGY ONE LIMITED, Research, Data, https://online.consciousinvestor.com/.
28. Conscious Investor, TECHNOLOGY ONE LIMITED, Research, Charts, https://online.consciousinvestor.com/.
29. Conscious Investor, WOOLWORTHS AND COCHLEAR LIMITED, Research, Charts, https://online.consciousinvestor.com/.
30. Conscious Investor, BHP LIMITED, Research, Charts, https://online.consciousinvestor.com/.
31. Conscious Investor, TECHNOLOGY ONE LIMITED AND TPG LIMITED, Research, Charts, https://online.consciousinvestor.com/.
32. Technology One Limited, *Annual Reports and presentations*, n.d., viewed 24 Nov 2021, https://technologyonecorp.com/company/investors/annual-reports#FY21; BHP, *Annual reporting: reflecting our long-term commitment to transparency*, n.d., viewed 24 Nov 2021, https://www.bhp.com/investors/annual-reporting.
33. Domino's Investors, *2021 Annual Report*, Domino's Pizza Enterprises Limited, 19 Aug 2021, viewed 25 Nov 2021, https://static1.squarespace.com/static/5bd052c7c46f6d0e23b11afb/t/611c3d1529157e71a8d4a9d4/1629240623784/FY21+Appendix+4E++Annual+Report.pdf.
34. Conscious Investor, DOMINO'S PIZZA ENTERPRISES LIMITED, Research, Charts, https://online.consciousinvestor.com/.
35. N Khadem, 'Virgin Australia owes almost $7b to more than 12,000 creditors', ABC News, ABC, 30 Apr 2020, viewed

23 Nov 2020, https://www.abc.net.au/news/2020-04-30/virgin-australia-owes-7-billion-creditors-meeting-administration/12198130.

36. M West, 'House of Cards: is Brookfield the next Babcock & Brown?', Michael West Media, 21 Oct 2019, viewed 23 Nov 2011, https://www.michaelwest.com.au/house-of-cards-is-brookfield-the-next-babcock-brown/; D John, 'ABC Learning "reliant" on debt to cover cash shortfalls', *The Sydney Morning Herald,* The Nine Group, 19 Mar 2010, viewed 23 Nov 2021, https://www.smh.com.au/business/abc-learning-reliant-on-debt-to-cover-cash-shortfalls-20100318-qiix.html.
37. P Knight, *Shoe Dog*, Simon & Schuster (UK), London, 2018.
38. Conscious Investor, TECHNOLOGY ONE LIMITED, Research, Charts, https://online.consciousinvestor.com/.
39. Quote Investigator, 'Compound Interest Is Man's Greatest Invention', 31 Oct 2011, viewed 23 Nov 2021, https://quoteinvestigator.com/2011/10/31/compound-interest/.
40. Berkshire Hathaway Inc, *Form 10-Q,* 30 Jun 2021, viewed 23 Nov 2021, https://berkshirehathaway.com/qtrly/links2ndqtr21.html.
41. D Allcot, 'Ready, Set, Pitch! Famous Investors' Best Advice on Finding Backers', *CO*, US Chamber of Commerce, https://www.uschamber.com/co/run/business-financing/tips-from-famous-investors.
42. Cochlear, 'Home', n.d., viewed 23 Nov 2021, https://www.cochlear.com/us/en/home.
43. Cochlear, 'About Graeme Clark', n.d., viewed 23 Nov 2011, https://www.cochlear.com/intl/about/company-information/history-of-innovation/about-graeme-clark.
44. Business Wire, 'Millward Brown, in Partnership with Jim Stengel, Reveals the 50 Fastest-Growing Brands in the World and Uncovers the Source of Their Success', Business

Wire Inc, 17 Jan 2012, viewed 23 Nov 2021, https://www.businesswire.com/news/home/20120117005066/en/Millward-Brown-Partnership-Jim-Stengel-Reveals-50.

45. M King, '4 lessons from the collapse of Forge Group', The Motley Fool Australia Pty Ltd, 17 Mar 2014, viewed 25 Nov 2021, https://www.fool.com.au/2014/03/17/4-lessons-from-the-collapse-of-forge-group/.
46. H Coleman and J Price, *Finding Wealth Winners the Teaminvest Way*, Teaminvest, Lindfield, 2020.
47. C Connley, 'Suzy Welch: Warren Buffett's simple career advice will transform how you approach your job', *CNBC Make It*, 23 Jan 2019, viewed 23 Nov 2021, https://www.cnbc.com/2019/01/18/warren-buffetts-career-advice-could-change-how-you-approach-your-job.html.
48. Berkshire Hathaway, *Berkshire's Corporate Performance vs. the S&P*, n.d., viewed 23 Nov 2021, https://www.berkshirehathaway.com/letters/2005ltr.pdf.
49. Berkshire Hathaway, *Berkshire's Corporate Performance vs. the S&P*, n.d., viewed 23 Nov 2021, https://www.berkshirehathaway.com/letters/2007ltr.pdf.
50. TED2018, 'How I climbed a 3,000-foot vertical cliff—without ropes' [online video], Presenter A Honnold, TED, Apr 2018, viewed 23 Nov 2021, https://www.ted.com/talks/alex_honnold_how_i_climbed_a_3_000_foot_vertical_cliff_without_ropes/transcript.
51. M Wakefield, '"If I get an adrenaline rush, something's gone wrong": An interview with Free Solo's Alex Honnold', *The Spectator*, The Spectator (1828) Ltd, https://spectatorworld.com/topic/adrenaline-free-solo-alex-honnold/.
52. J Berman, 'The Three Essential Warren Buffett Quotes to Live By', *Forbes*, Forbes Media LLC, 20 Apr 2014, viewed 23 Nov 2021, https://www.forbes.com/sites/jamesberman/2014/04/20/

the-three-essential-warren-buffett-quotes-to-live-by/#38d8f4265439.

53. D Saul, 'Buy When There's Blood in The Streets', *Forbes*, Forbes Media LLC, 23 Sept 2009, viewed 24 Nov 2021, https://www.forbes.com/2009/02/23/contrarian-markets-boeing-personal-finance_investopedia/#33102fb71799.
54. G. Bhutada, 'Purchasing Power of the U.S. Dollar Over Time', Visual Capitalist, 6 April 2021, viewed 25 Nov 2021, https://www.visualcapitalist.com/purchasing-power-of-the-u-s-dollar-over-time/.
55. B Collins, 'Here's What Warren Buffett's Mentor Said About Investing', *Forbes*, Forbes Media LLC, 7 Aug 2018, viewed 24 Nov 2021, https://www.forbes.com/sites/bryancollinseurope/2018/08/07/heres-what-warren-buffetts-mentor-said-about-investing/#7b2f1a224598.
56. Conscious Investor, TECHNOLOGY ONE LIMITED, Research, P/E Ratio Chart, https://online.consciousinvestor.com/.
57. Sharesight Portfolio Tracker, Sharesight, 2021, https://portfolio.sharesight.com/portfolios/527874#/share_search?consolidated=false&portfolio_id=527874.
58. StockCharts.com, 'Historical Chart Gallery of Market Indexes', n.d., viewed 24 Nov 2021, https://www.stockcharts.com/freecharts/historical/marketindexes.html.
59. J Buckingham, 'Why Market Volatility is your Friend', *Forbes*, Forbes Media LLC, 29 Jan 2015, viewed 24 Nov 2021, https://www.forbes.com/sites/johnbuckingham/2015/01/29/why-market-volatility-is-your-friend/#379e4922425d.
60. E Kaplan, 'Why Warren Buffett's "20-Slot Rule" will make you insanely successful and wealthy', *CNBC Make It*, CNBC LLC, 16 Mar 2017, viewed 24 Nov 2021, https://www.cnbc.com/2017/03/16/warren-buffetts-20-slot-rule-will-make-you-successful-and-wealthy.html.

61. J Wolinsky, 'Peter Lynch Investment Tips', ValueWalk LLC, 1 Jan 2018, viewed 24 Nov 2021, https://valuewalk.com/2018/01/peter-lynch-investments/.
62. N Taleb, *The Black Swan*, Random House, New York, 2010.
63. S Raza, 'Peter Lynch's Investing Principles and 25 Golden Rules', ValueWalk LLC, 22 Jul 2015, viewed 24 Nov 2021, https://valuewalk.com/2015/07/peter-lynchs-investing-principles-and-25-golden-rules.
64. Investment Master Class, 'Circle of Competence', ValueWalk LLC, 14 Nov 2016, viewed 24 Nov 2021, https://www.valuewalk.com/2016/11/circle-of-competence-quotes-2/.
65. TheStreet Staff, 'Definition of "VIX"', *TheStreet*, The Arena Group, 31 Dec 2018, viewed 24 Nov 2021, https://www.thestreet.com/dictionary/v/vix.

Made in the USA
Monee, IL
03 November 2026

67378086R00125